MY ADVENTURES AS A GERMAN SECRET SERVICE AGENT

CAPTAIN VON DER GOLTZ

Then Major in the Mexican Constitutionalist Army, from a photo taken at Juarez.
(On the left Lieutenant Leiva.)

MY ADVENTURES AS A GERMAN SECRET SERVICE AGENT

BY

CAPT. HORST VON DER GOLTZ

Formerly Major in the Mexican Constitutionalist Army, sometime Confidential Aide to Captain von Papen, Recalled Military Attaché to the Imperial German Embassy at Washington, German Secret Service Agent

With Sixteen Plates

The Naval & Military Press Ltd

Published by

The Naval & Military Press Ltd
Unit 10 Ridgewood Industrial Park,
Uckfield, East Sussex,
TN22 5QE England

Tel: +44 (0) 1825 749494
Fax: +44 (0) 1825 765701

www.naval-military-press.com
www.military-genealogy.com

In reprinting in facsimile from the original, any imperfections are inevitably reproduced and the quality may fall short of modern type and cartographic standards.

FOREWORD

I HAVE not striven to write an autobiography. This book is merely a summary—a sort of galloping summary—of the last ten years of my existence. As such, I venture to write it because my life has been bound up in enterprises in which the world is interested. It has been my fortune to be a witness and sometimes an actor in that drama of secret diplomacy which has been going on for so long and which in such a large way has been responsible for this World War.

There are many scenes in that drama which have no place in this book—many events with which I am familiar that I have not touched upon. My aim has been to describe only those things with which I was personally concerned and which I know to be true. For a full history of the last ten years my readers must go elsewhere; but it is my hope that these adventures of mine will bring them to a better understanding of the forces that have for so long been undermining the peace of the world.

Foreword

Inevitably there will be some who read this book who will doubt the truth of many of the statements in it. I cannot, unfortunately, prove all that I tell here. Wherever possible I have offered corroborative evidence of the truth of my statements; at other times I have tried to indicate their credibility by citing well recognised facts which have a direct bearing upon my contentions. But for the rest, I can only hope that this book will be accepted as a true record of facts which by their very nature are insusceptible of proof.

So far as my connection with the German Government is concerned, I may refer the curious to the British Parliamentary White Papers, Miscellaneous, Nos. 6 and 13, which contain respectively my confession and a record of the papers found in the possession of Captain von Papen, former Military Attaché to the German Embassy at Washington, and seized by the British authorities on January 2 and 3, 1916. There are also, in addition to the documents reproduced in this book, various court records of the trial of Captain Hans Tauscher and others in the spring of the same year. To German activities in the United States, the newspapers bear eloquent testimony. I have been concerned

Foreword

rather with the motives of the German Government than with a statement of what has been done. These motives, I believe, you will not doubt.

But there is one point which I must ask my readers not to overlook. I have told that I became a secret agent through the discovery of a certain letter which contained very serious reflections upon one of the most important personages in the world. I have told, also, how the possession of that letter had an important bearing upon the course of my life—how it led me to America, and how in the struggle for its possession I very nearly lost my life. This, I know, will be severely questioned by many. Before rejecting this part of my story, I ask merely that you consider the fate that overtook Koglmeier, the saddler of El Paso, whose only crime was that he had been partially in my confidence. I ask you to recall that another German, Lesser, who had been associated with me at the same time, mysteriously disappeared in 1915, shortly before von Papen left for Europe. No one has been able to prove why these men were treated as they were. And if I did not have in my possession *something* which the German Government regarded as highly important, why the surprising

Foreword

actions of that Government, actions none the less astonishing because they are well known and authenticated? Consider these things before you doubt.

Finally, let me say that I have taken the liberty of changing or omitting the names of various people who are mentioned in these adventures, merely because I have had no wish to compromise them by disclosing their identity.

NEW YORK, *July 8,* 1917.

CONTENTS

CHAPTER	PAGE

1. A MOMENTOUS DOCUMENT 1
   I find an old letter containing a strange bit of scandal—Its contents draw me into the service of the Kaiser.

2. DIAMOND CUT DIAMOND 17
   I impersonate a Russian Prince and steal a Treaty—What the Treaty contained and how Germany made use of the knowledge.

3. A BOTANIST IN THE ARGONNE . . . 39
   Of what comes of leaving important papers exposed—I look and talk indiscreetly, and a man dies.

4. "CHERCHEZ LA FEMME!" 55
   I am sent to Geneva and learn of a plot—How there are more ways of getting rid of a King than by blowing him up with dynamite.

5. THE STRONG ARM SQUAD 80
   Germany displays an interest in Mexico, and aids the United States for her own purposes—The Japanese-Mexican Treaty and its share in the downfall of Diaz.

6. A HERO IN SPITE OF MYSELF . . . 103
   My letter again—I go to America and become a United States soldier—Sent to Mexico and sentenced to death there—I join Villa's army and gain an undeserved reputation.

7. ENTER CAPTAIN VON PAPEN . . . 141
   War—I re-enter the German service and am appointed aide to Captain von Papen—The German conception of neutrality and how to make use of it—The plot against the Welland Canal.

Contents

CHAPTER	PAGE
8. MY INTERVIEW WITH THE KAISER . .	162

    I go to Germany on a false passport—Italy in the early days of the war—I meet the Kaiser and talk to him about Mexico and the United States.

9. MY ARREST AND CONFESSION . . . 179

    In England, and how I reached there—I am arrested and imprisoned for fifteen months—What von Papen's baggage contained—I make a sworn statement.

10. GERMANY'S HATE CAMPAIGN IN AMERICA . 200

    The German intrigue against the United States—Von Papen, Boy-Ed and von Rintelen, and the work they did—How the German-Americans were used and how they were betrayed.

11. MISCHIEF IN MEXICO 224

    More about the German intrigue against the United States—German aims in Latin America—Japan and Germany in Mexico—What happened in Cuba?

12. THE COMPLETE SPY 251

    The last stand of German intrigue—Germany's spy system in America—What is coming?

LIST OF ILLUSTRATIONS

CAPTAIN VON DER GOLTZ . . . *Frontispiece*	
	FACING PAGE
GROUP OF SOLDIERS OF THE MEXICAN CONSTITUTIONALIST ARMY	32
TELEGRAM FROM GEN. VILLA TO CAPT. VON DER GOLTZ	48
GROUP OF UNITED STATES RECRUITS IN VILLA'S ARMY—RAUL MADERO AND HIS STAFF . .	64
REPORT OF KOGLMEIER'S MURDER FROM THE *El Paso Herald*	80
GEN. VILLA AND COL. TRINIDAD RODRIGUEZ—GEN. RAUL MADERO	96
CAPT. VON DER GOLTZ'S COMMISSION AS MAJOR IN THE MEXICAN CONSTITUTIONALIST ARMY .	112
SIX MONTHS' LEAVE FROM GEN. RAUL MADERO TO CAPT. VON DER GOLTZ—GEN. RAUL MADERO'S LETTER OF RECOMMENDATION . . .	128
DR. KRASKE'S LETTER TO "BARON" VON DER GOLTZ	144
CAPT. VON PAPEN'S LETTER TO THE GERMAN CONSULS AT BALTIMORE AND ST. PAUL . . .	160
BILLS FROM THE DU PONT DE NEMOURS POWDER COMPANY FOR "MERCHANDISE" DELIVERED TO "BRIDGEMAN TAYLOR" AND CHARGED TO CAPT. TAUSCHER	176

List of Illustrations

	FACING PAGE
CAPT. TAUSCHER'S ORDER FOR "EXPLOSIVES"—HIS ACCOUNT TO CAPT. VON PAPEN FOR "MERCHANDISE"	192
PASSPORT ON WHICH CAPT. VON DER GOLTZ WENT TO GERMANY AND ENGLAND	208
SAFE-DEPOSIT RECEIPT FOR PAPERS WHICH CAPT. VON DER GOLTZ LEFT IN ROTTERDAM	224
THE ORDER FOR THE DEPORTATION OF CAPT. VON DER GOLTZ FROM THE UNITED KINGDOM	240
THE CHEQUE WHICH ALMOST COST CAPT. VON DER GOLTZ HIS LIFE	256

My Adventures as a German Secret Service Agent

CHAPTER I

A MOMENTOUS DOCUMENT

I find an old letter containing a strange bit of scandal, and its contents draw me into the service of the Kaiser.

ON March 29, 1916, the steamer *Finland* was warped into its Hudson River dock and I hurried down the gangway. I was not alone. Agents of the United States Department of Justice had met me at Quarantine; and a man from Scotland Yard was there also—a man who had attended me sedulously since, barely two weeks before, I had been released in rather unusual circumstances from Lewes prison in England; the last of four English prisons in which I had spent fifteen months in solitary confinement waiting for the day of my execution.

My friend from Scotland Yard left me very shortly; soon afterwards I was testifying for the United States Government against Capt. Hans

A Momentous Document

Tauscher, husband of Mme. Johanna Gadski, the diva. Tauscher, American agent of the Krupps and of the German Government, was charged with complicity in a plot to blow up the Welland Canal in Canada during the first month of the Great War. During the course of the trial it was shown that von Papen and others (including myself) had entered into a conspiracy to violate the neutrality of the United States. I had led the expedition against the Welland Canal, and I was telling everything I knew about it. Doubtless you remember the newspapers of the day.

You will remember how, at that time, the magnitude of the German plot against the neutrality of the United States became finally apparent. You will remember how, in connection with my exposure, came the exposure of von Igel, of Rintelen, of the German Consul-General at San Francisco, Bopp, and many others. With all these men I was familiar. In the activities of some of them I was implicated. It was I, as I have said, who planned the details of the Welland Canal plot. I shall tell the true story of these activities later.

But first let me tell the story of how I came to be concerned in these plots—and to do that I must go back over many years; I must

A Momentous Document

tell how I first became a member of the Kaiser's Secret Diplomatic Force (to give it a name) and incidentally I shall describe for the first time the real workings of that force.

I have been in and out of the Kaiser's web for ten years. I have served him faithfully in many capacities and in many places—all over Europe, in Mexico, even in the United States. I served the German Government as long as I believed it to be representing the interests of my countrymen. But from the moment that I became convinced that the men who made up the Government—the Hohenzollerns, the Junkers and the bureaucrats—were anxious merely to preserve their own power, even at the expense of Germany itself, my attitude towards them changed. That is why I write this book—and why I shall tell what I know of the aims and ambitions of these men—enemies of Germany as well as of the rest of the world.

I was not a spy; nor was I a secret service agent. I was, rather, a secret diplomatic agent. Let me add that there is a nice distinction between the three. A secret diplomatic agent is a man who directs spies, who studies their reports, who pieces together various bits of information,

A Momentous Document

and who, when he has the fabric complete, personally makes his report to the highest authority or carries that particular plan to its desired conclusion. His work and his status are of various sorts. Unlike the spy, he is a user, not a getter, of information. He is a freelance, responsible only to the Foreign Office; a plotter; an unofficial intermediary in many negotiations; and frequently he differs from an accredited diplomatic representative only in that his activities and his office are essentially secret. Obviously men of this type must be highly trained and trustworthy; and their constant association with men of authority makes it necessary that they, themselves, should be men of breeding and education. But above all, they must possess the courage that shrinks at no danger, and a devotion, a patriotism that know no scruples.

This, then, was the calling into which I found myself plunged, while still a boy, by one of the strangest chances that ever befell me, whose life has been full of strange happenings.

As I recall my adolescence I realise that I was a normal boy, vigorous, wilful, fond of sport, of horses, dogs and guns, and I know that but for the chance I speak of, I should have grown up in the traditions of our family—Cadet School

A Momentous Document

—the University—later a lieutenancy in the German Army—and to-day, perhaps, death "somewhere in France."

And yet, in that boyhood that I am recalling, I can remember that there were other interests which were far greater than the games that I loved, as did all lads of my age. Mental adventure, the matching of wits against wits for stakes of reputation and fortune, always exercised an uncanny fascination over my mind. That delight in intrigue was shown by the books I read as a boy. In the library of my father's house there were many novels, books of poems, of biography, travel, philosophy and history; but I passed them by unread. His few volumes of Court gossip and so-called "secret history" I seized with avidity. I used to bear off the memoirs of Maréchal Richelieu, the Cardinal's nephew, and read them in my room when the rest of the household was asleep.

I recall, too, that there was another tendency already developed in me. I see it in my dealings with other boys of that day. It was the impulse to make other people my instruments, not by direct command or appeal, but by leading them to do, apparently for themselves, what I needed of them.

A Momentous Document

Such was I, when my aunt, who had cared for me since the death of my parents some years before, fell ill and later died. I was disconsolate for a time and wandered about through the halls and chambers of the house, seeking amusement. And it was thus that one day I came upon an old chest in the room that had been hers. I remembered that chest. There were letters in it—letters that had been written to her by friends made in the old days when she was at Court. Often she had read me passages from them—bits of gossip about this or that personage whom she had once known—occasionally, even, mention of the Kaiser.

Doubtless, too, I thought, there were passages which she had not seen fit to read to me: some more intimate bits of gossip about those brilliant men and women in Berlin whom I then knew only as names. With the eager curiosity of a boy I sought the key, and in a moment had unlocked the chest.

There they lay, those neat, faded bundles, slightly yellow, addressed in a variety of hands. Idly I selected a packet and glanced over the envelopes it contained, lingering, in anticipation of the revelations that might be in them. I must have read a dozen letters before my eye

A Momentous Document

fell upon the envelope that so completely changed my life.

It lay in a corner of the chest, as if hidden from too curious eyes—a yellow square of paper, distinguished from its fellows by the quality of the stationery alone, and by its appearance of greater age. But I knew, before I had read fifty words of it, that I was holding in my hands a document that was more explosive than dynamite!

For this letter, written to my aunt years before, by one of the most exalted personages in all Germany, contained statements which, had they been made by anyone else, would have been treason to utter.

Those of you whose memories go back to the last twenty years of the nineteenth century, will readily recall the notorious ill-feeling that existed between Wilhelm II. and his mother, Victoria, the Dowager Empress Friedrich. Stories have so often been told of this enmity, culminating in the virtual banishment from Berlin of the Queen Mother, that I need not do more than mention them. But what is not so generally known is the small esteem in which Victoria was held by the entire German people. During the twenty years of her married life as the wife of the

A Momentous Document

then Crown Prince Friedrich, she was treated by Berlin Society with the most thinly veiled hostility. Even Bismarck made no attempt to conceal his dislike for her, and accused her—to quote his own words—of having "poisoned the fountain of Hohenzollern blood at its source."

Victoria, for her part, although she seems to have had no animosity towards the German people, certainly possessed little love for her eldest son, and did her best to delay his accession to the Imperial throne as long as she could. When in 1888 Wilhelm I. was dying, she tried her utmost to secure the succession to her husband, who was then lying dangerously ill at San Remo. "Cancer," the physicians pronounced the trouble, and even the great German specialist, Bergmann, agreed with their diagnosis. There is a law that prevents anyone with an incurable disease, such as cancer, from ascending the Prussian throne; but Victoria knew too well the attitude of her son, Wilhelm, towards herself, not to wish to do everything in her power to prevent him from becoming Emperor so long as she could. In her extremity she appealed to her mother, Queen Victoria of England, who sent Sir Morell Mackenzie, the great English surgeon, to San Remo to report on Friedrich's condition.

A Momentous Document

Mackenzie opposed Bergmann and said the disease was *not* cancer; and the physicians inserted a silver tube in the patient's throat, and in due course he became Emperor Friedrich III.

But in spite of Mackenzie and the silver tube, Friedrich III. died after a reign of ninety-eight days—and he died of cancer.

Now what was the reason for this hostility between mother and son and between Empress and subjects? There have been many answers given—Victoria's love for England, her colossal lack of tact, her impatient unconventionality. Berlin whispered of a dinner in Holland years before, when Victoria had entertained some English people she met there—people she had never seen before—and had finished her repast by smoking a cigar. That in the days when the sight of a woman smoking horrified the German soul! And Berlin hinted at worse unconventionalities than this.

As for the animosity of the Kaiser, this was attributed to the fact that he held her responsible for his withered left arm.

Plausible reasons, all of these, and possibly true. But consider, if you will, the rumours that followed Victoria all her life—the story of an early attachment to the Count Seckendorf, her

A Momentous Document

husband's associate during the Seven Weeks' War of 1866—the reports, sometimes denied but generally believed, of her marriage to the Count not long before her death. True or not, these stories—what does it matter?

But what to do with this letter to which I attached so much importance? Something impelled me not to speak of it to my family. But who else was there?

In my perplexity I did an utterly foolish thing. I put my whole confidence in a man's word. There was, serving at a nearby fortress, a Major-General von Dassel, who was in the habit of coming to our house quite regularly. To him I went, and under pledge of silence I told him my story. Of course, he broke the pledge and left immediately for Berlin. All doubts, if I had any, as to the importance of the document, vanished with him. And if I had any misgivings concerning my own importance they quickly vanished, too. Back from Berlin, with Major-General von Dassel came an agent of the Chancellor. He did not come to our house; instead von Dassel sent for me to go to his headquarters in the fortress. I met there a solemn frock-coated personage who, so he said, had come down from Berlin especially to see me. Imagine my

A Momentous Document

elation! I was in my element; what I had hoped for had at last happened. The pages of Richelieu and of my secret histories were coming true. Another man and I were to lock our wits in a fight to the finish—that pleasure I promised myself. He was a worthy opponent, an official, a professional intriguer. As I looked into his serious, bearded face, I built romances about him.

The agent of the Chancellor wanted my document and my pledge to keep silent about its contents. Through sheer love of combat, I refused him on both points. He tried persuasion and reason. I was adamant. He tried cajolery.

"It is plain," he said, in a voice that was caressingly agreeable, "that you are an extremely clever young man. I have never before met your like—that is, at your age. A great career will be possible to such a young man if only he shows himself eager to serve his Government, eager to meet the wishes of his Chancellor."

Of course, I was delighted with this flattery, which I felt was entirely deserved. I began to believe that I was a person of importance. I became stubborn—which always has been one of my best and worst traits. I saw that the gentleman in the frock-coat was becoming angry; his

A Momentous Document

serious eyes flashed. Apparently much against his will, he tried threats; he suavely pointed out that if I persisted in my resolve not to surrender the document, destruction yawned at my feet. The threats touched off the fuse of my romanticism. I felt I was leading the life of intrigue of which I had read.

"If you will wait here," I told him, "I shall go home and get the document for you."

The Chancellor's representative stroked his beard, deliberated a moment and seemed uncertain.

"Oh, the Junge will come back all right," put in Major-General von Dassel. But the boy did not come back. My family had always been excessively liberal with money, and I had enough in my own little "war chest" to buy a railway ticket, and a considerable amount besides. So I promptly ran off to Paris; and to this day I don't know how long the gentleman in the frock-coat waited for me in von Dassel's office.

The terrors and thrills and delight of that panic-stricken flight still make me smile. No peril I have since been through was half as exciting.... Berlin!... Köln!... Brussels! It was a keen race against arrest. I was

A Momentous Document

happily frightened, much as a colt is when it shies at its own shadow. Although I was in long trousers and looked years older than I was, I had not sense enough to see the affair in its true light —a foolish escapade which was quite certain to have disagreeable consequences. And so I fled from Berlin to Paris.

From Paris I fled too. There, any circumstance struck my fevered imagination as being suspicious. After a day in the French capital, I scurried south to Nice and from Nice to Monte Carlo. Precocious youngster, indeed, for there I had my first experience with that favoured figure of the novelist, the woman secret agent! No novelist, I venture to say, would ever have picked her out of the Riviera crowd as being what she was. She wore no air of mystery; and though attractive enough in a quiet way, she was very far from the siren type in looks or manners. The friendliness that she, a woman of the mid-thirties, showed a lonely boy was perfectly natural. I should never have guessed her to be an agent of the Wilhelmstrasse had she not chosen to let me know it. Of course, the moment she spoke to me of "my document," I knew she had made my acquaintance with a purpose. If the dear old frock-coated agent of the Chancellor had been

A Momentous Document

asleep, the telegraph wires from Berlin to Paris and Nice and Monte Carlo had been quite awake.

The proof that I was actually watched and waited for thrilled me anew. It also alarmed me when my friend explained how deeply my Government was affronted. Soon the alarm outgrew the thrill and in the end I quite broke down. Then the woman in her, touched with pity, apparently displaced the adventuress. We took counsel together and she showed me a way out.

"Your document," she said, "has a Russian as well as a German importance. Why not try St. Petersburg since Berlin is hostile? For the sake of what you bring, Russia might give shelter and protection."

Remember, I was very young and she was all kindness. Yes, she discovered for me the avenue of escape and she set my foot upon it in the most motherly way. And I unknowingly took my first humble lesson in the great art of intrigue. For, as I learned years afterwards, that woman was not a German agent but a Russian!

But at that time I was all innocent gratitude for her kindness. I was thankful enough to proceed to St. Petersburg by way of Italy, Constantinople and Odessa. Of course, she must have

A Momentous Document

designated a man unknown to me to travel with me, and make sure that I reached the Russian capital. To my hotel in St. Petersburg, just as the woman had predicted, came an officer of the political police, who courteously asked me not to leave the building for twenty-four hours. The next day the man from the Okrana, or Secret Police, came again. This time he had a droshky waiting, with one of those bull-necked, blue corduroy-robed, muscular Russian jehus on the box. We were driven down the Nevsky Prospekt to a palace. Here I soon found myself in the presence of a man I did not then know as Count Witte. He greeted me kindly, merely remarking that he had heard I was in some difficulties, and offering me aid and advice. My letter was not referred to and the interview ended.

So began the process of drawing me out. A fortnight later the matter of my information was broached openly and the suggestion was made that if I delivered it to the Russian Government, high officials would be friendly and a career assured me in Russia, as I grew up. But by that time Germany had changed her attitude. Her agents also reached me in St. Petersburg. From them I received a new assurance of the importance of the document. If I would release it—so the

A Momentous Document

German agent who came to my hotel told me—and keep my tongue still, Berlin would pardon my indiscretion and assure me a career at home. Russia or Germany? My decision was quickly made. That very night I was smuggled out of St. Petersburg and whisked across the frontier at Alexandrovna into Germany; and the letter passed out of my hands—for the time being.

CHAPTER II

DIAMOND CUT DIAMOND

I impersonate a Russian Prince and steal a Treaty—What the Treaty contained and how Germany made use of the knowledge.

GROSS LICHTERFELDE! As I write, it all comes back to me clearly, in spite of the full years that have passed—this, my first home in Berlin. A huge pile of buildings set in a suburb of the city, grim and military in appearance; and in fact, as I soon discovered.

I was to become a cadet, it seems; and where in Germany could one receive better training than in this same Gross Lichterfelde?

At home I had had some small experience with the exactions of the gymnasium; but now I found that this was so much child's play in comparison with the life at Gross Lichterfelde. We were drilled and dragooned from morning till night: mathematics, history, the languages—they were not taught us, they were literally pounded into us. And the military training! I am not unfamiliar with the curricula of Sandhurst, of St.

Diamond Cut Diamond

Cyr, even of West Point, but I honestly believe that the training we had to undergo was fully as arduous and as technical as at any of those schools. And we were only boys.

Military strategy and tactics; sanitation; engineering; chemistry; in fact, any and every study that could conceivably be of use to the future officers of the German Army; to all of these must we apply ourselves with the utmost diligence. And woe to the student who shirked!

Then there was the endless drilling, that left us with sore muscles and minds so worn with the monotony of it that we turned even to our studies with relief. And the supervision! Our very play was regulated.

Can you wonder that we hated it and likened the Cadet School to a prison? And can you imagine how galling it was to me, who had come to Berlin seeking romance and found drudgery?

But we learned. Oh, yes! The war has shown how well we learned.

There was one relief from the constant study which was highly prized by all the cadets at Gross Lichterfelde. It was the custom to select from our school a number of youths to act as pages at the Imperial Court; and lucky were the ones who were detailed to this service. It meant a

Diamond Cut Diamond

vacation, at the very least, to say nothing of a change from the Spartan fare of the school.

I must have been a student for a full three months before my turn came; long enough, at any rate, for me to receive the news of my selection with the utmost delight. But I had not been on service at the Imperial Palace for more than a few days when a State dinner was given in honour of a guest at Court. He was a young prince of a certain grand-ducal house, which by blood was half Russian and half German. I recall the appearance of myself and the other pages, as we were dressed for the function. Ordinarily we wore a simple undress cadet uniform, but that evening a striking costume was provided: nothing less than a replica of the garb of a mediæval herald—tabard and all—for Wilhelm II. has a flair for the feudal. From my belt hung a capacious pouch, which, pages of longer standing than I assured me, was the most important part of my equipment; since by custom the ladies were expected to keep these pouches comfortably filled with sweetmeats. Candy for a cadet! No wonder every boy welcomed his turn at page duty, and went back reluctantly to the asceticism of Gross Lichterfelde.

That was my first sight of an Imperial dinner.

Diamond Cut Diamond

The great banquet hall that overlooks the square on the Ufer was ablaze with lights. The guests—the men in their uniforms even more than the women—made a brilliant spectacle to the eyes of a youngster from the provinces; but most brilliant of all was Wilhelm II., resplendent in the full dress uniform of a field-marshal. I can recall him as he sat there, lordly, arrogant, yet friendly, but never seeming to forget the monarch in the host. It seemed to me that he loved to disconcert a guest with his remarks; it delighted him to set the table laughing at someone else's expense.

By chance, during the banquet, it fell to me to render service to the young Emperor. Once, as I moved behind his chair, a German Princess exclaimed, "Oh, doesn't the page resemble his Highness?"

The Kaiser looked at me sharply.

"Yes," he agreed, "they might well be twins." Then, impulsively lifting up his glass, he flourished it towards the Russo-German prince and drank to him.

That was all there was to the incident—then. I returned to Gross Lichterfelde the next morning, and proceeded to think no more of the matter. Nor did it come to my mind when a few weeks

Diamond Cut Diamond

later, I was suddenly summoned to Berlin, and driven, with one of my instructors, to a private house in a street I did not know. (It was the Wilhelmstrasse, and the residence stood next to Number 75, the Foreign Office. It was the house Berlin speaks of as Samuel Meyer's Bude—in other words, the private offices of the Chancellor and His Imperial Majesty.)

We entered a room, bare save for a desk or two and a portrait of Wilhelm I., where my escort surrendered me to an official, who silently surveyed me, comparing his observations with a paper he held, which apparently contained my personal measurements. Later a photograph was taken of me, and then I was bidden to wait. I waited for several hours, it seemed to me, before a second official appeared—a large, round-faced man, soldierly despite his stoutness—who greeted my escort politely and, taking a photograph from his pocket, proceeded to scrutinise me carefully. After a moment he turned to my escort.

"Has he any identifying marks on his body?" he asked.

My escort assured him that there was none.

"Good!" he exclaimed; and a moment later we were driving back towards Gross Lichterfelde —I quite at sea about the whole affair, but not

Diamond Cut Diamond

daring to ask questions about it. Idle curiosity was not encouraged among cadets.

I was not to remain in ignorance for long, however. A few days later I was ordered to pack my clothing, and with it was transferred to a quiet hotel in the Dorotheenstrasse. The hotel was not far from the War Academy, and there I was placed under the charge of an exasperatingly exacting tutor, who strove to perfect me on but three points. He insisted that my French should be impeccable; he made me study the private and detailed history of a certain Russian house; and he was most particular about the way I walked and ate, about my knowledge of Russian ceremonies and customs—in a word, about my deportment in general.

The weeks passed. At last, by dint of much hard work, I became sufficiently expert in my studies to satisfy my tutor. I was taken back to the house in the Wilhelmstrasse, where the round-faced man again inspected me. He talked with me at length in French, made me walk before him and asked me innumerable questions about the family history of the house I had been studying. Finally he drew a photograph from his pocket—the same, I fancy, which had figured in our previous interview.

Diamond Cut Diamond

"Do you recognise this face?" he inquired, offering me the picture.

I started. It might have been my own likeness. But no! That uniform was never mine. Then in a moment I realised the truth and with the realisation the whole mystery of the last few weeks began to be clear to me. The photograph was a portrait of the young Prince Z——, my double, whom I had served at the banquet.

"It is a very remarkable likeness," said the round-faced man. "And it will be of good service to the Fatherland."

He eyed me for a moment impressively before continuing.

"You are to go to Russia," he told me. "Prince Z—— has been invited to visit his family in St. Petersburg, and he has accepted the invitation. But unfortunately Prince Z—— has discovered that he cannot go. You will, therefore, become the Prince—for the time being. You will visit your family, note everything that is said to you and report to your tutor, Herr ——, who will accompany you and give you further instructions.

"This is an important mission," he added solemnly, "but I have no doubt that you will comport yourself satisfactorily. You have been

Diamond Cut Diamond

taught everything that is necessary; and you have already shown yourself a young man of spirit and some discretion. We rely upon both of these qualities." He bowed in dismissal of us, but as we turned to go he spoke again.

"Remember," he was saying, "from this day you are no longer a cadet. You are a prince. Act accordingly."

That was all. We were out of the door and half way to our hotel before I realised to the full the great adventure I had embarked upon. Embarked? Shanghaied would be the better term. I had had no choice whatsoever in the matter. I had not even uttered a word during the interview.

At any rate, that night I left for Petrograd—still St. Petersburg at that time—accompanied by my tutor and two newly engaged valets, who did not know the real Prince. Of what was ahead I had no idea, but as my tutor had no doubts of the success of our mission, I wasted little time in speculating upon the future.

What the real prince's motive was in agreeing to the masquerade, and where he spent his time while I was in Russia, I have never been able to discover. From what followed, I surmise that he was strongly pro-German in his sympathies,

Diamond Cut Diamond

but distrusted his ability to carry through the task in hand.

In St. Petersburg I discovered that my "relatives"—whom I had known to be very exalted personages—were inclined to be more than hospitable to this young kinsman whom they had not seen for a long time. I found myself petted and spoiled to a delightful degree; indeed I had a truly princely time. The only drawback was that, as the constant admonitions of my tutor reminded me, I could spend my princely wealth only in such ways as my—shall I say, prototype?—would have done. He, alas, was apparently a graver youth than I.

So two weeks passed, while I was beginning to wish that the masquerade would continue indefinitely, when one day my tutor sent for me.

"So," he said, "we have had play enough, is it not so? Now we shall have work."

In a few words he explained the situation to me. Russia, it seemed, was about to enter into an agreement with England regarding spheres of influence in Persia. Already a certain Baron B—— (let me call him) was preparing to leave St. Petersburg with instructions to find out in what circumstances the British Government would

Diamond Cut Diamond

enter into *pourparlers* on the subject. Berlin, whose interests in the Near East would be menaced by such an agreement, needed information—and delay. I was to secure both. It was the old trick of using a little instrument to clog the mechanism of a great machine.

Let me explain here a feature of the drawing up of international treaties and agreements which, I think, is not generally understood. Most of us who read in the newspapers that such and such a treaty is being arranged between the representatives of two countries, believe that the terms are even then being decided upon. As a matter of fact these terms have long since been determined by other representatives of the two countries concerned, and the present meeting is merely for the formal and public ratification of a treaty already secretly made. The usual stages in the making of a treaty are three: First, an unofficial inquiry by one Government into the willingness or unwillingness of the other Government to enter into a discussion of the question at issue. This is usually done by a man who has no official standing as a diplomat at the moment, but whose relations with officials in the second country have given him an influence there which will stand his Government in good stead. After

Diamond Cut Diamond

a willingness has been expressed by both sides to enter into discussions, official *pourparlers* are held in which the terms of the agreement are discussed and decided upon. Finally, the treaty is formally ratified by the Foreign Ministers or special envoys of the countries involved. Secrecy in the first two stages is necessitated by the fear of meddling on the part of other Governments, and also by a desire on the part of any country making overtures to avoid a possible rebuff from the other; and it explains why negotiations which are publicly entered into never fail.

But to return to my adventures. My Government had learned of the impending *pourparlers* between Britain and Russia; it knew that Baron B——'s instructions would contain the conditions which Russia considered desirable. What was necessary was to secure these instructions.

Now, my tutor had, long before this, seen to it that I should be on friendly terms with various members of the Baron's household; and he had been especially insistent that I should pay a good deal of attention to the young daughter of the house, whom I shall call Nevshka. I had wondered at the time why he should do this; but I obeyed his instructions with alacrity. Nevshka was charming.

Diamond Cut Diamond

Soon I saw the purpose of this carefully fostered friendship.

"The Baron will spend this evening at the club," I was informed. "He will return, according to his habit, promptly at twelve. You will visit his house this evening, paying a call upon Nevshka. You will contrive to set back the clock so that his home-coming will be in the nature of a surprise to her. The hour will be so late that she, knowing her father's strictness, will contrive to get you out of the house without his seeing you. That is your opportunity! You must slip from the salon into the rear hall—but do not leave the house. And if, young man, with such an opportunity, you cannot discover where these papers are hidden *and secure them*, you are unworthy of the trust that your Government has placed in you."

I nodded my comprehension. In other words I was to take advantage of Nevshka's friendship in order to steal from her father—I was to perform an act from which no gentleman could help shrinking. And I was going to do it with no more qualms of conscience than, in time of war, I should have felt about stealing from an enemy general the plan of an attack.

For countries are always at war—diplomatic-

Diamond Cut Diamond

ally. There is always a conflict between the foreign ambitions of Governments; always an attempt on the part of each country to gain its own ends by fair means or foul. Every man engaged in diplomatic work knows this to be true. And he will serve his Government without scruple, for well he knows that some seemingly dishonourable act of his may be the means of averting that actual warfare which is only the forlorn hope that Governments resort to when diplomatic means of mastery have failed.

So I undertook my mission with no hesitation, rather with a thrill of eagerness. I pretended to be violently interested in Nevshka (no difficult task, that) and time sped by so merrily that even had I not turned back the hands of the clock, I doubt whether the lateness of the hour would have seriously concerned either of us. Oh, yes, my tutor—who, as you of course have guessed by now, was no mere tutor—had analysed the situation correctly.

As the Baron was heard at the door, I drew out my watch.

"Nevshka, your clock is slow. It is already midnight."

Nevshka started.

"Come!" she exclaimed. "Father must not

Diamond Cut Diamond

see you. He would be furious at your being here at this hour." In a panic she glanced about the salon. "Go out that way!" And she pointed to a door at the rear, one that opened on a dimly lit hall.

I went. I heard the Baron express his surprise that Nevshka was still awake. I heard her lie—beautifully, I assure you. And I remained hidden while the Baron worked in his library for a while; scarcely daring to breathe until I heard him go up the stairs to his bedroom.

He was a careless man, the Baron. Or perhaps he had been reading Poe, and believed that the most obvious place of concealment was the safest. At any rate, there in a drawer of his desk, protected only by the most defenceless of locks, were the papers—a neat statement of the terms upon which Russia would discuss this Persian matter with England.

I returned home with my prize, to find my tutor awaiting me. He said no word of commendation when I gave him the papers, but I knew by his expression that he was well pleased with my work. And I went to bed, delighted with myself, and dreaming of the great things that were to come.

Next day we left St. Petersburg. A German

Diamond Cut Diamond

resident of the city had telephoned my relatives, warning them that a few cases of cholera had appeared. Would it not, he suggested (Oh, it was mere kind thoughtfulness on his part!), be best to let the young prince return to Germany until the danger was over? His parents would be worried. Indeed, it would be best, my "relatives" agreed. So with regret they bade me good-bye; and in the most natural manner in the world I returned to Berlin.

Wilhelmstrasse 76 again! The round-faced man again, but this time less military, less unbending, in his manner. I had done well, he told me. My exploit had attracted the favourable attention of a very exalted personage. If I could hold my tongue—who knows what might be in store for me?

That was the end of the matter, so far as I was concerned. But in the history of European politics it was only the beginning of the chapter.

It may be well, at this point, to recall the political situation in Europe, as it affected England, Russia and Germany at the time. Even two years before—in 1905—it had become evident to all students of international affairs that the next great conflict, whenever it should come,

Diamond Cut Diamond

would be between England and Germany; and England, realising this, had already begun to seek alliances which would stand between her and German ambitions of world dominance. The Entente with France had been the first step in the formation of protective friendships; and although this friendship had suffered a strain during the Russo-Japanese War, because of the opposing sympathies of the two countries, the end of the war healed all differences. The defeat of Russia removed all immediate danger of a Slav menace against India. To England, then, the weakened condition of Russia offered an excellent opportunity for an alliance that would draw still more closely the "iron ring round Germany." Immediately she took the first steps towards this alliance.

Now, Russia stood badly in need of two things. War-torn and threatened by revolution, the Government could rehabilitate itself only by a liberal amount of money. But where to get it? France, her ally, and normally her banker, was slow in this instance to lend—and it was only through England's intervention that the Tsar secured from a group of Paris and London bankers the money with which to finance his Government and stave off revolution.

GROUP OF SOLDIERS OF THE MEXICAN CONSTITUTIONALIST ARMY (See p. 115)

Diamond Cut Diamond

But more than money, Russia needed an ice-free seaport to take the place of Port Arthur, which she had lost; and for this there were only two possible choices : Constantinople or a port on the Persian Gulf. In either of these aims she was opposed by Britain, the traditional enemy of a Russian Constantinople, on the one hand, and the possessor of a considerable "sphere of interest" in the Persian Gulf on the other.

So matters stood, when in August, 1907, *but a few weeks after my masquerade,* an Agreement was signed, providing for the division of Persia into three strips, the northern and southern of which would be respectively Russian and British zones of influence; providing also, in a secret clause, that *Russia would give England military aid in the event of a war between Germany and England!*

Meantime what was Germany doing?

She had, you may be sure, no intention of allowing England to best her in the game of intrigue. Her interests in the Near East were commercial rather than military; but she could not see them threatened by an Anglo-Russian occupation of Persia. Then, too, she was bound to consider the possible effect on Turkey, in

Diamond Cut Diamond

which she was taking an ever-increasing (and none too altruistic) interest.

The details of what followed I can only surmise. I know that in the interval between my trip to Russia and the signing of that Agreement, on August 31, the Kaiser held two conferences: one on August 3, with the Tsar at Swinemünde; the other on August 14, with Edward VII., at the Castle of Wilhelmshöhe. And when, on September 24, the terms were published, they were bitterly attacked by a portion of the English Press, not so much because of the danger to Persia, as because of the fact that Russia got the best of the bargain!*

Had the Kaiser succeeded in having these terms changed? Who knows? Certainly one can trace the hand of German diplomacy in the events of the next seven years, most of which are a matter of common knowledge. The steady aggressions of Russia in Persia during the troubled years of 1910-1912; the almost open flouting of the terms of the treaty, which expressly guaranteed Persian integrity; the constant growth of German influence, culminating in the Persian extension of the German-owned

* You will find an interesting account of the effect of this treaty upon Persia in William Morgan Shuster's valuable book, "The Strangling of Persia."

Diamond Cut Diamond

Bagdad Railway; the founding of a German school and a hospital in Teheran, jointly supported by Germany and Persia; and finally, the celebrated Potsdam Agreement of 1910, between Russia and Germany, in which Germany agreed to recognise Russia's claim to Northern Persia as its sphere of influence, which provided for a further *rapprochement* between the two countries in the matter of railway construction and commercial development generally, and which has been generally supposed to contain a guarantee that neither country would join "any combination of Powers that has any aggressive tendency against the other."

And England did not protest, in spite of the fact that the Potsdam Agreement absolutely negatived her own treaty with Russia and made it, in the language of one writer, " a farce and a deception!" Why? Was it because she believed that when war came, as it inevitably must, Russia would forget this new alliance in allegiance to the old?

England was mistaken if she believed so. Russia—Imperial Russia—was never so much the friend of Germany as when, neglecting the war on her own Western front, she sent her armies into the Caucasus, persuaded the British to

Diamond Cut Diamond

undertake the Dardanelles expedition, and, following her own plans of Asiatic expansion, betrayed England!

As I write Kut-el-Amara is creating a great stir in the Allied countries. The Indian Government has been severely blamed for sending General Townshend into Mesopotamia with insufficient material, medical supplies and troops. The official explanation was that the force was employed in order to protect the oil pipes supplying the British Navy in those waters from being destroyed by the enemy. There was no doubt in my mind at the time, in spite of the fact that I was in prison and communication with the outside was very meagre, that this was not the real reason. Subsequent developments have shown—and the abandonment of the inquiry instituted by the British Government about this affair only further supports my contention—that Russia intended to use England's helpless position to secure for herself an access to the Persian Gulf. The Grand Duke Nicholas himself abandoned the campaign on the Eastern front to go to the Caucasus. The Gallipoli enterprise which turned out to be such a monumental failure was undertaken upon his instigation. Do you think for one second that if Imperial Russia had thought England was able to

Diamond Cut Diamond

capture Constantinople, a city which she herself had been wanting for centuries, she would have invited England to do so? The fact is that the Gallipoli enterprise tied up all England's available reserves so that the English could practically do nothing to forestall Russian movements to the Persian Gulf. The Government of India, realising the danger, sent General Townshend upon the famous Bagdad campaign rather as a demonstration than as a military enterprise. I will quote from my diary which I kept while in prison:

"Just read in the *Times*: 'British moving north into Mesopotamia to protect oil pipes and capture Bagdad.' I don't need to read *Punch* any more, the *Times* being just as funny. My dear friends, you didn't move up there for that reason. You went up there so as to be able to tell your Russian friends that there was no need to come farther south as you were there already."

That is the story of my little expedition into Russia—and of what it brought about.

As for me, I was sent back to Gross Lichterfelde, where I abruptly ceased to be a young prince, and became once more a humble cadet. But only to outside eyes. Dazzled by the success of my first mission, I regarded myself as a Super-

Diamond Cut Diamond

man among the cadets. Life loomed romantically before me. I told myself that I was to consort with princes and beautiful noblewomen and to spend money lavishly. The future seemed to promise a career that was the merriest, maddest for which a man could hope.

I laugh sometimes now when I think of the dreams I had in those days. I was soon to learn that the life which Fate had thrust upon me was set with traps and pitfalls which might not easily be escaped. I was to learn many lessons and to know much suffering; and I was to discover that the finding of my " document " was only the beginning of a chain of events that were to control my whole life—and that its influence over my career had not ended.

But at that time I was all hopes and rosy dreams—of my future, of myself, occasionally of Nevshka.

Nevshka! Is she still as charming as ever?

CHAPTER III

A BOTANIST IN THE ARGONNE

Of what comes of leaving important papers exposed—I look and talk indiscreetly, and a man dies.

IN spite of my dreams and extreme self-satisfaction, I found the atmosphere of Gross Lichterfelde as drab and monotonous as ever it had been before my masquerade. Discipline sits lightly upon one who is accustomed to it solely, but to me, fresh from a glorious fortnight of intrigue and festivity, it was doubly galling. Yet there was one avenue of escape open to me that was denied my fellows, for I was required to pay a weekly visit to my tutor in the Wilhelmstrasse, there to continue my studies in the art of diplomatic intrigue.

It is a significant comment upon the life at Gross Lichterfelde that I could regard these visits as a kind of relaxation. Surely no drillmaster was ever so exacting as this tutor of mine. And yet, despite his dryness and the complete lack of cordiality in his manner, there was somewhere the gleam of romance about him. To me

A Botanist in the Argonne

he seemed, in a strangely inappropriate way, an incarnation of one of those old masters of intrigue who had been my heroes in former days at home; and my imagination distorted him into a gigantic, shadowy being, mysterious, inflexible and potentially sinister.

We studied history together that autumn; not the dull record of facts that was forced upon us at Gross Lichterfelde, but rather a history of glorious national achievement, of ambitions attained and enemies scattered—a history that had the tone of prophecy. And I would sit there in the soft autumn sunlight viewing the Fatherland with new eyes; as a knight in shining armour, beset by foes, but ever triumphing over them by virtue of his righteousness and strength of arm.

Then I would return to Gross Lichterfelde and its discipline.

Yet even at Gross Lichterfelde we contrived to amuse ourselves, chiefly by violating regulations. That is generally the result of walling any person inside a set of rules; his attention becomes centred on getting outside. American cadets at West Point, so I have been told, have their traditional list of devilries, maintained with admirable persistence in the face of severe penal-

A Botanist in the Argonne

ties. At Gross Lichterfelde one proved his manliness by breaking bounds at least once a week to drink beer and flirt with maids none the less divine because they were hopelessly plebeian.

In the prevailing lawlessness I bore my share, and in the course of my escapades I formed an offensive and defensive alliance with a cadet of my own age against that common enemy of all our kind, the Commandant of the school. Willi von Heiden I will call my chum, because that was not his name. We became close friends. And through our friendship there came an event which I shall remember to my last day. It gave me a glimpse into the terrible pit of secret diplomacy.

Often at the present I find myself living it over in my mind. If I have learned to take a lighter view of life than most men, my attitude dates from that time when a careless word of mine, spoken in innocence, condemned a man to death. I will try to tell very briefly how it came about.

The Christmas after my excursion to St. Petersburg I was invited by Willi von Heiden to visit him at his home. His father was a squireling of East Prussia, one of the Junkers. He had an estate in that rolling farm land between

A Botanist in the Argonne

Goldap and Tilsit, which was the scene of countless adventures of Willi's boyhood.

Just before we left Gross Lichterfelde—yes, even there they allow you a few days' vacation at Christmas—Willi received a letter and came to me with a joyous face.

"Good news!" he cried, "we are sure to have a lively holiday. Brother Franz is getting a few days' leave too."

I had heard much of Willi's older brother, Franz. He was a young man in the middle twenties, an officer of a famous fighting regiment of foot, one of the Prussian Guards. Willi had dilated upon him in his conversation with me. Franz was his younger brother's hero. From all accounts Franz von Heiden was possessed of a mind of that rare sort which combines unremitting industry with cleverness. His future as a soldier seemed brilliant and assured.

"Where is Franz?" was Willi's first question when we reached home.

I shall be long forgetting my first impressions of the man. I had been looking for a dry, spectacled student, or a stiff young autocrat of the thoroughly Prussian type, which I, like many other Germans, thoroughly disliked and inwardly laughed at. Instead, I found another chum.

A Botanist in the Argonne

Franz was an engaging young man of slight build, but very vigorous and athletic. I found him frank, friendly, unassuming, apparently wholly care-free and full of quiet drollery. From his first greeting any prejudice that I might have formed from hearing my chum Willi chant his excellences was quite wiped away. And as the days passed I found myself drawn to seek Franz's company constantly. I have no doubt it flattered my vanity—always awake since my exploit in St. Petersburg—to find this older man treating me as a mental equal. It seemed to me that he differentiated between me and Willi, who was quite young in manner as well as years. At times the impulse was very strong in me to confide in Franz, to let him know that I was not a mere cadet, that I had been in Russia for my Government. Luckily for myself I suppressed that impulse—luckily for me, but very unluckily for Lieutenant Franz von Heiden, as it turned out.

One sunny December morning we were all three going out rabbit shooting. While Willi counted out cartridges in the gun-room I went to summon Franz from the bedroom he was using as his study. It was characteristic of him that without any assumption of importance he gave

A Botanist in the Argonne

a few hours to work early every morning, even while on leave. I found him intent upon some large sheets of paper, but he pushed them aside.

"Time to start now?" he asked. "Good! Wait a minute, while I dress." He stepped into the adjoining dressing-room.

And then, as if Fate had taken a hand in the moment's activities, I did a thing which I have never ceased to regret. Fate! Why not? What is the likelihood that by mere vague chance I, of all the cadets of Gross Lichterfelde, should have become Willi von Heiden's chum and shared his holidays? That by mere chance I should have been an inmate of his home when Franz was there, three days out of the whole year? That by mere chance I, with my precocious knowledge and thirst for yet more knowledge, should have entered his study when he was occupied with a particular task? Why did I not send the servant to call him? And why, instead of doing any one of the dozen other things I might have done while I was waiting for Franz to change his clothes, should I have stepped across and looked at the big sheets of paper on his table?

I did just that. I did it quite frankly and without a thought of prying. I saw that the

A Botanist in the Argonne

sheets were small-scale maps. They were the maps of a fort, and the names upon them were written both in French and in German. The thrill of a great discovery shot all through me. It flashed upon me that I had heard Willi say that during the previous summer Franz had spent a long furlough in the Argonne section of France. He had been fishing and botanising—so Willi had said. Indeed, only the night before Franz himself had told us stories of the sport there; and all his family had accepted the stories at their face value. So had I until that moment when I stood beside his desk and saw the plans of a French field fortress. Then I knew the truth. Lieutenant Franz von Heiden was doing important work—so confidential that even his family must be kept in ignorance about it—for the Intelligence Department of the German General Staff. Like me, he was entitled to the gloriously shameful name of spy!

If I had obeyed my natural impulse to rush into Franz's room and exchange fraternal greetings with this new colleague of the secret service, so romantically discovered, he might have saved himself. Instead, something made me play the innocent and be the innocent, too, as far as intent was concerned.

A Botanist in the Argonne

When Franz returned, dressed for the shoot, I was standing looking out of his window, and I said nothing about my discovery.

We had our rabbit shoot that day. We crowded all the fun and energy possible into it. It was our last day together, and by sundown I felt as close to Franz von Heiden as though he were my own brother. A few days later Willi and I went back to Gross Lichterfelde.

Shortly after I returned from my Christmas leave my tutor sent for me. He even recognised the amenities of the occasion enough to unbend a little and greeted me with a trace of mechanical friendliness.

"I trust you had a pleasant holiday," he said; "you told me, did you not, that you were to spend it at the Baron von Heiden's?"

That touch of friendliness was the occasion of my tragic error. I remember that I plunged into a boisterous description of my vacation, of the pleasant days in the country, of the shooting, of Franz. As my tutor listened, with a tolerant air, I told him what a splendid fellow Franz was, how cleverly he talked and how diligently he worked. And then, with a rash innocence for which I have never forgiven myself, I told him of what I had seen on that day of the rabbit

A Botanist in the Argonne

shooting—of the maps on the table. Franz was one of us!

But my tutor was not interested. Abruptly he interrupted my burst of gossip; and soon after that he plunged me into an exam. in spoken French. My progress in that seemed his only preoccupation.

A month later Willi von Heiden staggered into my room. "Franz is dead!" he said.

The brilliant young lieutenant, Franz von Heiden, had come to a sudden and shocking end. He was shot dead in a duel. His opponent was a brother officer, a Captain von Frentzen. The "Court of Honour" of the regiment had approved of the duel and it was reported that the affair was carried out in accordance with the German code.

Later I learned the story. Captain von Frentzen was suddenly attached to the same regiment as Franz. His transfer was a cause of great surprise to the officers and of deep displeasure to them, for the captain had a notorious reputation as a duellist. Naturally the officers, Franz among them, had ignored him, trying to force him out of the regiment. Upon the night of a regimental dance the situation came to a head.

In response to the gesture of a lady's fan Franz crossed the ball-room hurriedly. He was

A Botanist in the Argonne

caught in a sudden swirl of dancers and accidentally stepped on Captain von Frentzen's foot. In the presence of the whole company von Frentzen dealt Franz a stinging slap in the face.

"Apparently," he sneered, "you compel me to teach you manners!"

Franz looked at him, amazed and furious. There was nothing that he had done which warranted von Frentzen's action. It was an outrage—a deadly insult. There was but one thing to do. A duel was arranged.

To understand more of this incident you must understand the unyielding code of honour of the German officer. Franz von Heiden's original offence had been so very slight that even had he refused to apologise to Frentzen the consequences might not have been serious. But Frentzen's blow given in public was quite a different matter. It was a mortal affront. I heard that Franz's captain had been in a rage about it.

"My best lieutenant!" he had said to the colonel. "An extremely valuable man. To be made to fight a duel with that worthless butcher, von Frentzen. Shameful! God knows that laws are sometimes utterly unreasonable judged by many of our ideas, as officers are equally senseless. I have racked my brain to find a way out of this

WESTERN UNION TELEGRAM

THEO. N. VAIL, PRESIDENT

RECEIVED AT Main Office, 608-610 So. Spring Street, Los Angeles, Cal.

1074

153CAB 9

ELPASO TEX NOV 22 1913

BARON HORST VON DERGOLTZ
GERMAN CONSULATE LOSANGELES CAL

DR RACHBAUM PROPOSITION ACCEPTED COME WITH THE NEXT TRAIN

GENERAL VILLA

2PM

TELEGRAM FROM GENERAL VILLA TO CAPTAIN VON DER GOLTZ. (See p. 118)

A Botanist in the Argonne

difficulty, but it seems impossible. Can't you do something to interfere?"

The colonel looked at him steadily. "Your honest opinion; is von Heiden's honour affected by Frentzen's action?"

There was nothing Franz's captain could do but reply "Yes."

The duel was held on the pistol practice grounds of the garrison, a smooth, grassy place, surrounded by high bushes; at the lower end there was a shed built of strong boards, in which tools and targets were stored. At daybreak Franz von Heiden and his second dismounted at the shed and fastened their horses by the bridle. They stood side by side, looking down the road, along which a carriage was coming. Captain von Frentzen, his second, and the regimental surgeon got out. Sharp polite greetings were exchanged. On the faces of the seconds there was a singular expression of uneasiness, but Frentzen looked as though he were there for some guilty purpose. The prescribed attempts at reconciliation failed. The surgeon measured off the distance. He was a long-legged man and made the fifteen paces as lengthy as possible.

Just at this moment the sun came up fully. Pistols were loaded and given to Franz and Frent-

A Botanist in the Argonne

zen. Fifteen paces apart the two men faced each other. One of the seconds drew out his watch, glanced at it and said, "I shall count; ready, one! then three seconds; two!—and again three seconds; then, stop! Between one and stop the gentlemen may fire."

He glanced round once more. The four officers stood motionless in the level light of the dawn. He began to count. Presently Franz von Heiden was stretched out upon the ground, his blue eyes staring up into the new day. He lay still. . . .

When I heard that story I ceased to be a boy. My outlook on the future had been that of an irresponsible gamester, undergoing initiation into the gayest and most exciting sports. All at once my eyes were hideously opened and I looked down into the pit that the German secret service had prepared for Franz von Heiden, and knew I *was the cause of it.* It was terrible! By leaving that map where I could see it Franz von Heiden had been guilty of an unforgivable breach of trust. By his carelessness he had let someone know that the Intelligence Department of the General Staff had procured the plans of a French fortress in the Argonne. Wherefore, according to the iron law of that soulless war machine, Franz von Heiden must die.

A Botanist in the Argonne

And this is the sinister way it works. Trace it! I innocently betray him to my tutor, an official of the Secret Diplomatic Service. A few days later one of the deadliest pistol shots in the German army is transferred to Franz's regiment. A duel is forced upon him and he is shot down in cold blood.

Not long after the news of the duel, my tutor sent for me. "Is it not a curious coincidence," he began, his cold grey eyes boring into mine, "that the last time you were here we spoke of Lieutenant Franz von Heiden? The next time you come to see me he is dead. I understand that certain rumours are in circulation about the way he died. Some of them may have already come to your notice. I caution you to pay no attention whatever to such silly statements. Remember that a Court of Honour of an honourable regiment of the Prussian Guards has vouched for the fact that Lieutenant von Heiden's quarrel with Captain von Frentzen and the unfortunate duel that followed were conducted in accordance with the officers' code of the Imperial Army."

I hung my head, sick at heart; but he was relentless.

"Remember also," he said in a pitiless voice, "that men of intelligence never indulge in fruit-

A Botanist in the Argonne

less gossip, even among themselves. I hope you understand that—by now." He paused a moment, as if he remembered something.

"For some time," he went on, in the most casual way, "I have been aware that it will be necessary for me to talk to you seriously. Now is as good a time as any. You know that your training for your future career has been put largely in my hands. I am responsible for your progress. The men who have made me responsible require reports about your development. They have not been wholly satisfied with what I was able to tell them. Your intentions are good. You show a certain amount of natural cleverness and adaptability, but you have also disappointed them by being impulsive and indiscreet.

"Now," he said, "I ask you to pay the closest attention to everything I shall say. Your attitude must be changed if you are to go on and some day be of service to your Government. You must learn to treat your work as a deadly serious business—not as a romantic adventure. We were just speaking of von Heiden. I seem to remember vaguely that the last time you were here you had some sort of a cock-and-bull story to tell me of—what was it?—of seeing some secret maps of French fortifications on the unfortunate young

A Botanist in the Argonne

man's table. I could hardly refrain from smiling at the time. Such insanity! You do not imagine for a moment, do you, that if he had proved himself discreet enough to be entrusted with such highly confidential things, he would have been so imprudent as to betray that fact to a mere casual friend of his little brother? I hope you see how absurd such imaginings are."

I groaned mentally as he continued:

"Remember now," my tutor said icily, "every man in our profession is a man who not only knows very much, but may know too much, unless he can be trusted to keep what he knows to himself. There are three ways in which he can fail to do that—by carelessness, by accident, and by deliberate talking. Never talk—never be careless—never have accidents happen to you. Then you will be safe, and in no other way can you be so safe. Keep that in your mind! You will find it much more profitable and useful than remembering what anybody has to say about Franz von Heiden. It was a commonplace quarrel with Captain von Frentzen which killed him. A Court of Honour has said so."

That night at Gross Lichterfelde, after lights were out, Willi von Heiden came creeping to my bed. I was the only intimate friend he had

A Botanist in the Argonne

there, and he felt the need of talking with someone about the big brother who had been his hero. Need I go into details of how his artless confidence made me feel? But human beings are exceedingly selfish and self-centred creatures. I had a heartfelt sorrow for my chum and his family in their tragic bereavement. And, blaming myself as I did for it, I was abased completely. Yet there was another feeling in me at least as deeply rooted as these two emotions. It was dread.

Dread was to follow me for many years. I had learned the dangers of the dark secret world in which I lived. Its rules of conduct and its ruthless code had been revealed to me, not merely by precept but by example. And with that realisation all the thrill of romance and adventure disappeared. For I knew that I, too, might at any time be counted among the men who " knew too much."

CHAPTER IV

"CHERCHEZ LA FEMME!"

I am sent to Geneva and learn of a plot—How there are more ways of getting rid of a King than by blowing him up with dynamite.

IF at any time in this story of my life I have given the impression that accident did not play a very important part in the work of myself and other secret agents, I have done so unintentionally. "If" has been a big word in the history of the world; and even in my small share of the events of the last ten years, chance has oftentimes been an abler ally than some of the best-laid of my plans. If, for instance, I had not happened to be in Geneva in the winter of 1909-10; or if a certain official of the Russian secret police—the Okrana—had not met a well-deserved death at the hands of a committee of "Reds"; or if the German Foreign Office had not been playing a pretty little game of diplomacy in the south-western corner of Europe—why, the world to-day would be poorer by a King, and possibly richer by another combatant in the Great War.

"Cherchez la Femme!"

And if another King had not kept a diary he might have kept his throne. And if both he and a certain young diplomat, whose name I think it best to forget, had not had a common weakness for pretty faces, Germany would have lost an opportunity to gain some information that was more or less useful to her, a certain actress would never have become famous, and this book would have lost an amusing little comedy of coincidences.

All of which sounds like romance and is—merely the truth.

I had spent two uneventful years at Gross Lichterfelde at the time the comedy began; two years of study in which I had acquired some knowledge and a great weariness of routine, of hard work unpunctuated by any element of adventure. Of late it had almost seemed as if, after all, it was planned that I should become merely one of the vast army of officers that Gross Lichterfelde and similar schools were yearly turning out. For such a fate, as you can imagine, I had little liking.

Consequently I was far from displeased when one day I received a characteristically brief note from my old tutor, asking me to call upon him. Still more was I elated when, the next day, he

"Cherchez la Femme!"

informed me that I had had enough of books for the time being, and that he thought a little practical experience would be good for me. A vacation, I might call it, if I wished—with a trifle of detective work thrown in.

H'm! I was not so delighted with that prospect, and when the details of the " vacation " were explained to me, I was strongly tempted to say "No" to the entire proposition. But one does not say "No" to my old tutor. And so, in the course of a week, I found myself spending my evenings in the Café de l'Europe in Geneva, bound on a quiet hunt for Russian revolutionists.

Russia, at this time, had not quite recovered from the fright she received in 1905 and 1906, when, as you will remember, popular discontent with the Government had assumed very serious proportions. "Bloody Sunday," and the riots and strikes that followed it, were far in the past now, it is true, but they were still well remembered. And although most of the known revolutionary leaders had been disposed of in one way or another, there were still a few of them, as well as a large number of their followers, wandering in odd corners of Europe. These it was thought best to get rid of; and Russian agents began ferreting them out. And Germany—always less

"Cherchez la Femme!"

unfriendly to the Romanoffs than has appeared on the surface—lent a helping hand.

So it happened that on a particular night in December of 1909 I sat in the Café de l'Europe, bitterly detesting the work I had in hand, yet inconsistently wishing that something would turn up. I had no idea at the moment what I should do next. Chance rumour had led me to Geneva, and I was largely depending upon Chance for further developments.

They came. I had been sitting for an hour, I suppose, sipping vermouth and lazily regarding my neighbours, when the sound of a voice came to my ears. It was the voice of a man speaking French, with the soft accent of the Spaniard; the tone loud and unsteady and full of the boisterous emphasis of a man in his cups. But it was the words he spoke that commanded my attention.

"Our two comrades," he was saying, "will soon arrive from the centre in Buenos Ayres."

"Yes," another voice assented—a harsher voice, this, to whose owner French was obviously also a foreign tongue. "In the spring, we hope."

The Spaniard laughed.

"An excellent business! So simple. Boom! And our dear Alfonso——"

"Cherchez la Femme!"

Some element of caution must have come over him, for his voice sank so that I could no longer hear his words. But I had heard enough to make me assume a good deal.

Someone was to be assassinated! And that someone? It was a guess, of course, but the name and the accent of the speaker were more than enough to lead me to believe that the proposed victim must be King Alfonso of Spain.

I sat there, undecided for the moment. It was really no affair of mine. I was on another mission, and, after all, my theory was merely a supposition. On the other hand, the situation presented interesting possibilities—and, as I happened to know, Alfonso's seemingly pro-German leanings had made him an object of friendly interest at that time to my Government.

I decided to look into the matter.

It had been difficult to keep from stealing a glance at my talkative neighbours, but I restrained myself. I must not turn around, and yet it was vitally necessary to see their faces. All I could do was to hope that they would leave before I finished my vermouth; for I had no mind to risk my clearheadedness with more than the glass I had already had.

They did leave shortly afterwards. As they

"Cherchez la Femme!"

passed my table I took care to study their faces, and my intention to keep them in sight was immensely strengthened. The Spaniard I did not know, but his companion I recognised as a Russian —*and one of the very men I was after.*

I had been in Geneva long enough to know where I could get information when I needed it. It was only a day or two, therefore, before I had in my hands sufficient facts to justify me in reporting the matter to my Government.

Alfonso was in England at the time and presumably safe; for I had gathered that no attempt would be made upon his life until he returned to Spain. So I wrote to Berlin mentioning what I had learned.

A telegram reached me next day. I was ordered to Brussels to communicate my information to the Spanish Minister there.

Mark that! I was ordered to Brussels, although there was a Spanish Minister in Switzerland. But my Government knew that there were many factions in Spain, and it had strong reasons to believe that the Spanish Minister to Belgium was absolutely loyal to Alfonso. And in a situation such as this, one takes as few risks as possible.

I followed my instructions. The Spanish Minister thanked me. He was more than inter-

"Cherchez la Femme!"

ested; and he begged me, since I had no other direct orders, to do him the personal favour of staying a few days longer in the Belgian capital. I did so, of course, and a day or so later received from my Government instructions to hold myself at the Spaniard's disposal for the time being.

One night, at the Minister's request, I met him and we discussed matters fully. He wished me, he said, to undertake a more thorough investigation of the plot. I was already involved in it, and would be working less in the dark than another. Besides, he hinted, he could not very well employ an agent of his own Government. Who knew how far the conspiracy extended?

I was not displeased to abandon my chase of the Russian revolutionaries, for whom I felt some sympathy. So, as a preliminary step, I went to Paris, where, through the good offices of one Carlos da Silva—a young Brazilian freethinker who was there ostensibly as a student—I succeeded in gaining admission into one of the fighting organisations of Radicals there. They were not so communicative as I could have wished, but by judicious pumping I soon learned that there was an organised conspiracy against the life of Alfonso, and that the details of the plot were in the hands of a committee in Geneva.

"Cherchez la Femme!"

Geneva, then, was my objective point. But what to do if I went there? I knew very well that conspirators do not confide their plans to strangers. And I dared not be too inquisitive. Obviously the only course to follow was to employ an agent.

Now "Cherchez la femme" is as excellent a principle to work on when you are choosing an accomplice, as it is when you are seeking the solution of a crime. I therefore proceeded to seek a lady—and found her in the person of a pretty little black-eyed "revolutionist," who called herself Mira Descartes, and with whom I had already had some dealings.

It is here that accident crosses the trail again. For if a certain official of the Okrana had not been murdered in Moscow three years before, his daughter would never have conceived an intense hatred of all revolutionary movements and I should have been without her invaluable assistance in the adventure I am describing.

Mira Descartes! She was the kind of woman of whom people like to say that she would have made a great actress. Actress? I do not know. But she was an artist at dissembling. And she had beauty that turned the heads of more than the "Reds" upon whom she spied; and a genius

"Cherchez la Femme!"

for hatred: a cold hatred that cleared the brain and enabled her to give even her body to men she despised in order the better to betray them.

I was fortunate in securing her aid, I told myself; and I did not hesitate to use her services. (For in my profession, as must have been apparent to you, scrupulousness must be reserved for use "in one's private capacity as a gentleman.")

So Mlle. Descartes went to Geneva and, armed with my previously acquired information and her own charms, she contrived to get into the good graces of the committee there, and surprised me a week later by writing to Paris that she had already contracted a liaison with the Spaniard whom I had overheard speaking that night in the Café de l'Europe.

Soon I had full information about the entire plot. It was planned, I learned, to blow up King Alfonso with a bomb upon the day of his return to Madrid. The work was in the hands of two South Americans who were then in Geneva.

But far more important than this was the information which Mlle. Descartes had obtained that a high official of Spain—a member of the

"Cherchez la Femme!"

Cabinet—was cognizant of the plot and had kept silent about it.

Why, I asked myself, should this official—a man who surely had no sympathy with the aims of the revolutionists—lend his aid to them in this plot? The reason was not hard to discover. Alfonso's position at the time was far from secure. His Government was unpopular at home; and the pro-Teutonic leanings of many officials had lost him the moral and political support of the English Government and Press—facts of considerable importance.

So it seemed possible that Alfonso's reign might not be of long duration. And the new Government? It might be Radical or Conservative; pro-English or pro-German. A man with a career did well to keep on friendly terms with all factions. Thus, I fancied, the Cabinet Minister must have reasoned. At any rate he said nothing of the plot.

But I went to Brussels and reported all I had learned—and did not forget to mention the Cabinet Minister's rumoured share in the plot.

There my connection with the affair ceased. But not long afterwards a little tragi-comedy occurred which was a direct result of my activities. Let me recall it to you.

RAUL MADERO AND HIS STAFF
Captain von der Goltz stands second from left. (*See p.* 139)

GROUP OF UNITED STATES RECRUITS IN VILLA'S ARMY
Captain von der Goltz at the extreme left. (*See p.* 11?)

"Cherchez la Femme!"

On the evening of May 24, 1910, those of the people of Madrid who were in the neighbourhood of the monument which had been raised in memory of the victims of the attempted assassination of Alfonso, four years before, were horrified by a tragedy which they witnessed.

There was a sudden commotion in the streets, an explosion, and the confused sound of a crowd in excitement.

What had happened? Rumour ran wild throughout the crowd. The King was expected home that day—he had been assassinated. There had been an attempted revolution. Nobody knew any details.

But the next day everybody knew. A bomb had burst opposite the monument—a bomb that had been intended for the King. One man had been killed; the man who carried the bomb. But the King had not arrived in Madrid that day, after all.

The police set to work upon the case and presently identified the dead man as José Tasozelli, who recently arrived in Spain from Buenos Ayres. It was not certain whether he had any accomplices.

And while the police worked, the King—following a secret arrangement which had been

"Cherchez la Femme!"

made by the Spanish Minister at Brussels, and of which not even the Cabinet had been informed —arrived safely and quietly in Madrid; a day late, but alive.

What became of the Cabinet Minister? There are no autocracies now, and not even a King may prosecute without proof. So the Minister escaped for the time being. But it is interesting to remember that this same Minister was assassinated not a great while afterwards.

Now there are more ways of getting rid of a king than by blowing him up with dynamite. Foreign Offices are none too squeamish in their methods, but they do balk at assassination, even if the proposed victim is a particularly objectionable opponent of their plans. There is another method which, if correctly followed, is every bit as efficacious. Again I must refer you to that excellent French maxim: "Cherchez la femme."

It would be difficult to estimate properly the part that women have played in the game of foreign politics. As spies they are invaluable: for amorous men are always garrulous. But as enslavers of Kings they are of even greater service to men who are interested in effecting a change of dynasty. Even the most loyal of sub-

"Cherchez la Femme!"

jects dislikes seeing his King made ridiculous; and in countries where the line is not too strictly drawn between the public exchequer and the private resources of the monarch, a discontented faction may see some connection between excessive taxes and the jewels that a demi-mondaine wears. Revolutions have occurred for less than that—as every Foreign Office knows.

I am not insinuating that all royal scandals are to be laid at the door of international politics. I merely suggest that, given a king who is to be made ridiculous in the eyes of his subjects, it is a simple matter for an interested Government to see that he is introduced to a lady who will produce the desired effect. But no diplomat will admit this, of course. Not, that is, until after he has "retired."

This brings me to the second act of my comedy.

If I were drawing a map of Europe—a diplomatic map—as it was in the years of 1908 to 1910, I should use only two colours. Germany should be, let us say, black; England red. But the black of Germany should extend over the surfaces of Austria, Italy and Turkey; while France and Russia should be crimson. The rest of the Continent would be of various tints, ranging from a discordant combination of red and

"Cherchez la Femme!"

black, through a pinkish grey, to an innocuous and neutral white.

In the race to secure protective alliances against the inevitable conflict, both Germany and England were diligently attempting to colour these indeterminate territories with their own particular hue. Not least important among the courted nations were Spain and Portugal. Both were traditionally English in sympathy; both had shown unmistakable signs, at least so far as the ruling classes were concerned, of transferring their friendship to Germany. It was inevitable, therefore, that these two countries should be the scene of a diplomatic conflict which, if not apparent to the outsider, was fought with the utmost bitterness by both sides.

Somehow, by good fortune rather than any other agency, Spain had managed to avoid a positive alliance with either nation. Alfonso was inclined to be pro-German at that time; but an adroit juggling of the factions in his kingdom had prevented him from using his influence to the advantage of Germany.

Portugal was in a different situation. Poorer in resources than her neighbour, and hampered by the necessity of keeping up a colonial empire which in size was second only to England's, she

"Cherchez la Femme!"

had greater need of the protection of one of the Powers. Traditionally—and rightly from a standpoint of self-interest—that Power should have been England. There were but three obstacles to the continuance of the friendship that had existed since the Peninsular War—King Manoel, the Queen Mother and the Church.

Germany seemed all-powerful in the Peninsula in 1908. Alfonso's friendship was secured, and the boy king of Portugal was completely under the thumb of a pro-German mother and a Church which, as between Germany and England, disliked Germany the less. England realised the situation, and in approved diplomatic fashion set about regaining her ascendancy.

But diplomacy failed. At the end of two years Berlin was more strongly entrenched in Portugal than ever; and England knew that only heroic measures could save her from a serious diplomatic defeat.

Then Manoel did a foolish thing. He kept a diary.

It was a commonplace diary, as you will remember if you read the parts of it which were published some time after the revolution which dethroned its author. But there were portions of it—many of them never published—which ex-

"Cherchez la Femme!"

pressed beyond doubt Manoel's anti-English feeling and his affection for Germany.

Somehow England obtained possession of the diary. In October, 1910, Manoel fled to England, where he hoped against hope that the Government would live up to that provision of the treaty of 1908 which pledged England to aid the Portuguese throne in the event of a revolution.

But England—remembering the diary—wisely forgot its pledge. And a Republican Government in Portugal looked with suspicion upon the diplomatic advances of a nation which had been too friendly towards the exiled king—and became pro-English, as you know.

There ends my comedy. But there is an amusing epilogue to the affair, which was not without its importance to the Wilhelmstrasse, and in which I had a small part. To tell it I must pass over several months of work of one sort or another, until I come to the following winter—that of 1911.

I was on a real vacation this time and had selected Nice as an excellent place in which to spend a few idle but enlivening weeks. The choice was not a highly original one, but as it turned out, Chance seemed to have had a hand in it, after all. Almost the first person I met

"Cherchez la Femme!"

there was a man with whom I had been acquainted for several years, and who was destined to have his share in the events which followed.

People who have travelled in Europe much can hardly have avoided seeing upon one occasion or another a famous riding troupe who called themselves "the Bishops." They were five in number—Old Bishop, his daughter and her husband, a man named Merrill, and two others—and their act, which was variously known as "An Afternoon on the Bois de Boulogne," "An Afternoon in the Tiergarten," etc. (according to the city in which they played), was a feature of many of the noted circuses of seven or eight years ago. At this time they were helping to pay their expenses in the winter by playing in a small circus which was one of the current attractions of Nice.

I had bought horses from old Bishop in the past and knew him for a man of unusual shrewdness who, besides being the father of a charming and beautiful daughter, was in himself excellent company; and I was consequently pleased to run across him and his family at a time when all my friends seemed to be in some other quarter of the earth. We talked of horses together, and it was suggested that I might care to inspect an Arab

"Cherchez la Femme!"

mare, a recent acquisition, of which the old man was immensely proud.

That evening I heard of the arrival in Nice of a young British diplomat whom, I remembered, I had once met at a hotel in Vienna. I called upon him the following day—but I did so, not so much to renew our old acquaintance, as because that very morning I had received a rambling letter from my chief commenting upon the imminent arrival of the Englishman, and suggesting that I might find him a pleasant companion during my stay on the Riviera.

More work, in other words. My chief did not waste time in encouraging purposeless friendships. As I read the letter, it was a hint that the Englishman had something which Berlin wanted and I was to get it.

It was not difficult to recall myself to the Under-Secretary. We became friendly, and proceeded to " do " Nice together; and in the course of our excursions we became occasional visitors at the villa of an Eastern Potentate.

The Potentate in question was an engaging and eccentric old gentleman, who had been an uncompromising opponent of the English during his youth in India, and was now practically an exile, spending most of his time in planning

"Cherchez la Femme!"

futile conspiracies against the British Government, which he hated, and making friends with Englishmen, against whom he had no animosity whatever. He was especially well disposed towards my diplomatic friend, and the two spent many a riotous evening together over the chess board, at which the Potentate was invariably successful.

Meanwhile I made various plans and cultivated the acquaintance of the latter's secretary. He was a Bengali, who might well have stepped out of Kipling, so far as his manner went. In character the resemblance was not so close. I happened to know that he was paid a comfortable amount yearly by the British Government, to keep them informed of his master's movements; and I also happened to know that the German Government paid him a more comfortable amount for the privilege of deciding just what the British Government should learn. (I have often wondered whether he shared the proceeds with the Potentate, and whether even he knew for whom he was really working.) The secretary, I decided, might be of use to me.

As it happened, it was the secretary who unwittingly suggested the method by which I finally gained my object. It was he who commented

"Cherchez la Femme!"

upon the diplomat's intense interest in the Potentate's seraglio, giving me a clue to the character of the Englishman which was of distinct service. And it was he who suggested one evening that the three of us—for the Potentate was ill at the time—should attend a performance of the circus in which my friends, the Bishops, were playing.

You foresee the end, no doubt. The too susceptible diplomat was infatuated by Mlle. Bishop's beauty and skill. He wished to meet her, and I, who obligingly confessed that I had had some transactions with her father, undertook to secure the lady's permission to present him to her.

I did secure it, of course, although not without considerable opposition on the part of all three of the family; for circus people are very straight-laced. However, by severely straining my purse and my imagination, I convinced them that they would be doing both a friendly and a profitable act by participating in the little drama that I had planned. Eventually they consented to aid me in discomfiting the diplomat, whom I represented as having in his possession some legal papers that really belonged to me, although I could not prove my claim to them.

You will pardon me if I pass over the events

"Cherchez la Femme!"

of the next few days and plunge directly into a scene which occurred one night, about a week later, the very night, in fact, on which the Bishops were to close their engagement with the little circus in which they were playing. It was in the sitting-room of the diplomat's suite at the hotel that the scene took place; dinner à *deux* was in progress—and the diplomat's guest was Mlle. Bishop, who had indiscreetly accepted the Englishman's invitation.

Came a knock at the door. Mademoiselle grew pale.

"My husband!" she exclaimed.

Mademoiselle was right. It was her husband who entered—very cold, very business-like, and carrying a riding crop in his hand. He glanced at the man and woman in the room.

"I suspected something of the sort," he said, in a quiet voice. "You are indiscreet, Madame. You do not conceal your infidelities with care." He took a step towards her, but paused at an exclamation from the Englishman.

"Do not fear, Monsieur"—elaborate irony was in his voice as he addressed the diplomat—"I shall not harm you. It is with this—lady—only that I am concerned. She has, it appears, an inadequate conception of her wifely duty. I must,

'Cherchez la Femme!"

therefore, give her a lesson." As he spoke he tapped his boot suggestively with his riding whip.

"My only regret," he continued politely, "is that I must detain you as a witness of a painful scene, and possibly cause a disturbance in your room."

Again he turned towards his wife, who had sat watching him with a terrified face. Now as he approached her she burst into tears, and ran to where the Englishman stood.

"He is going to beat me," she sobbed. "Help me, for Heaven's sake! Stop him! Give him—give him anything!"

But the Englishman did not need to be coached.

"Look here!" he cried suddenly, interposing between the husband and wife. "I'll give you fifty pounds to get out of here quietly. Good God, man, you can't do a thing like this, you know! It's horrible. And you have no cause. I give you my word you have no cause."

He was a pitiable mixture of shame and apprehension as he spoke. But Merrill looked at him calmly. He was quite unmoved and still polite when he replied:

"The word of a gentleman, I suppose! No,

"Cherchez la Femme!"

Monsieur, it is useless to try to bribe me. It is a great mistake, in fact. Almost "—he paused for a moment, as if he found it difficult to continue—" almost it makes me angry."

He was silent for a space, but when he spoke again it was as if in response to an idea that had come to him.

"Yes," he continued, "it does make me angry. Nevertheless, Monsieur, I shall accept your suggestion. Madame and I will leave quietly, and in return you shall give us—oh, not money—but something that you value very much."

He turned to his wife.

"Madame, you will go to Monsieur's trunk, which is open in the corner, and remove every article so that I can see it."

The Englishman started. For a moment it seemed as if he would attack Merrill, who was the smaller man, but fear of the noise held him back. Meanwhile, the woman was rifling the trunk, holding up each object for her husband's inspection. The latter stood at the door, his eyes upon both of the others.

"We are not interested in Monsieur's clothing," he said calmly. "What else is there in the trunk? Nothing? The desk then! Only some papers? That is a pity. Let me have them,

"Cherchez la Femme!"

however—all of them. And you may give me the portfolio that lies on the bureau."

As he took the packet the rider turned to the diplomat, who stood as if paralysed in the corner of the room.

"I do not know what is in these papers, Monsieur, but I judge from your agitation that they are valuable. I shall take them from you as a warning—a warning to let married women alone in future. Also I warn you not to try to bribe a man whom you have injured. You have made me very angry to-night by doing so.

"Above all," he added, "I warn you not to complain to the police about this matter. This is not a pretty story to tell about a man in your position—and I am prepared to tell it. Good night, Monsieur!"

He did not wait to hear the Englishman's reply.

That night, while the two younger members of the Bishop family sped away by train—to what place I do not know—and old Bishop expressed great mystification over their disappearance, I made a little bonfire in my grate of papers which had once been the property of the diplomat, and which I knew would be of no interest to my

"Cherchez la Femme!"

Government. There were a few papers which I did not burn—a memorandum or two, and a bulky typewritten copy of Manoel's diary, which I found amusing reading before I took it to Berlin.

I called upon my English friend the next day, but I did not see him. He had fallen ill and been obliged to leave Nice immediately. No; it was impossible to say what the ailment was.

"Ah, well," I thought, as I returned to my room, "he will get over it."

It was an embarrassing loss, but not a fatal one; and doubtless he could explain it satisfactorily at home.

I was sorry for him, I confess. But more than once that day I laughed as I thought of the scene of last night, as Mlle. Bishop had described it to me. An old game—but it had worked so easily.

But then, wasn't it Solomon who complained about the lack of original material on this globe?

The diary? I took it to Berlin, as I have said, where it was a matter of considerable interest. Subsequently it was published, after discreet editing.

But at that time I was engaged upon a matter of considerably more importance.

CHAPTER V

THE STRONG ARM SQUAD

Germany displays an interest in Mexico, and aids the United States for her own purposes—The Japanese-Mexican Treaty and its share in the downfall of Diaz.

It was in Paris that my next adventure occurred. I had gone there following one of those agreeably indefinite conversations with my tutor which always preceded some especial undertaking. "Why not take a rest for a few weeks?" he would say. "You have not seen Paris for some time. You would enjoy visiting the city again—don't you think so?" And I would obligingly agree with him—and in due course would receive whatever instructions were necessary.

It may seem that such methods are needlessly cumbersome and a little too romantic to be real; but, in fact, there is an excellent reason for them. Work such as mine is governed too greatly by emergencies to admit of definite planning beforehand. A contingency is foreseen—faintly, and as a possibility only—and it is thought advisable to have a man on the scene. But until that con-

Fighting For His Life; Koglmeier Is Murdered

Harnessmaker Is Found Dying in His Shop, With Many Evidences of a Desperate Struggle; Had Been Beaten Over the Head With Some Blunt Instrument; Robbery Theory Is Abandoned.

AFTER apparently struggling desperately with his assailants, E. E. Koglmeier, aged 52 years, volunteer fireman and pioneer El Pasoan, was murdered in his place of business, 319 South Santa Fe street, some time between the hours of 7:30 and 9 oclock Saturday night. Five jagged cuts and holes, some of them being located in the back of the head, and four wounds of a similar nature inflicted on the face, resulted in his death. Life was all but extinct when Mr. Koglmeier was found lying in a pool of blood about the center of the room of his harness and saddlery shop. He was, in his shirt sleeves Robbery is not believed to have been the motive for the crime.

William Gieseler, a merchants' policeman, was the first one to discover Mr. Koglmeier. He had passed the shop on his first round at 7 oclock Saturday night when it is said that he spoke to Mr. Koglmeier. Returning to the shop on his second round at 9:15 oclock Gieseler saw the door of the open. Gieseler walked in. He presentiment that something wrong. The glare from the flashlight disclosed the b Koglmeier. He was it was evi minute me?

removed to a local undertaking establishment.

Evidences of a Struggle.

Despite the fact that the first blow evidently had been delivered when his back was turned to his murderers, Mr. Koglmeier must have struggled before he was beaten down for the last time. Trails of blood ran from almost every section of the room, showing that the struggle had been long before the victim was finally compelled to succumb from the blows dealt him with either a dull hatchet or some iron instrument.

Theory of the Crime.

The belief is that two men called at the harness shop a little after 7 oclock. They had gone there under the pretense of making a purchase. Bridles ness and collars hang suspend the ceiling of the place, murderers had evidentl horse collar as the

REPORT OF KOGLMEIER'S MURDER FROM THE *EL PASO HERALD* FOR DECEMBER 22nd, 1913.

(*See p.* 131)

The Strong Arm Squad

tingency develops into an assured fact, it would be the sheerest waste of energy to give an agent definite instructions which might have to be changed at any moment.

So I had become accustomed to receive my instructions in hints and stingy morsels, understanding perfectly that it was part of my task to discover for myself the exact details of the situation which confronted my Government. If I were not sufficiently astute to perceive f r myself many things which my superiors would never tell me—well, I was in the wrong profession, and the sooner I discovered it the better.

I went to Paris in just that way and put up at the Grand Hotel. So far as I knew I was on genuine leave of absence from all duties and I proceeded to amuse myself. Though under no obligations to report to anyone, I did occasionally drop around to the Quai d'Orsay—where most of the embassies and consulates are—to chat with men I knew. One day it was suggested to me at the German Embassy that I should lunch alone the next day at a certain table in the Café Américaine.

"I would suggest," said one of the secretaries, "that you should wear the black derby you have on. It is quite becoming"—this with

The Strong Arm Squad

an expressionless face. "I would suggest also that you should hang it on the wall behind your table, not checking it. Take note of the precise hook upon which you hang it. It may be that there will be a man at the next table who also will be wearing a black derby hat, which he will hang on the hook next to yours. When you go out be careful to take down his hat instead of your own."

I asked no questions. I knew better. Old and well known as it is, the "hat trick" is perennially useful. Its very simplicity makes it difficult of detection. It is still the best means of publicly exchanging documents between persons who must not be seen to have any connection with each other.

I went to the Café Américaine, that cosmopolitan place on the Boulevard des Italiens near the Opera. My man had not yet come, I noticed, and I took my time about ordering luncheon, drank a "bock" and watched the crowd. Near by was a party of Roumanians, offensively boisterous, I thought. An American was lunching with a dancer then prominent at the Folies. Two Englishmen—obviously officers on leave—chatted at another table, and in a corner, a group of French merchants heatedly discussed some

The Strong Arm Squad

business deal. The usual scene—almost commonplace in its variety.

Slowly I finished luncheon, and when I turned to get my hat, I saw, as I expected, that there was another black derby beside it. I took the stranger's derby, and when I reached my room in the Grand Hotel I lifted up the sweat band. There on thin paper were instructions that took my breath away. For the time being I was to be in charge of the "Independent Service" of the German Government in Paris—that is, the Strong Arm Squad.

This so-called "Independent Service" is an interesting organisation of cut-throats and thieves whose connection with diplomatic undertakings is of a distinctly left-handed sort, and is, incidentally, totally unsuspected by the members of the organisation themselves. Composed of the riff-raff of Europe—of men and women who will do anything for a consideration and ask no questions—it is frequently useful when subtler methods have failed and when by violence only can some particular thing be accomplished. As an organisation the "Independent Service" does not actually exist: the name is merely a generic one applied for convenience to the large number of people in all great cities who are available for such

The Strong Arm Squad

work, and who, if they fail and are arrested or killed, can be spared without risk or sorrow.

Naturally in illegal operations the trail must not lead to the Embassy; and for that reason all transactions with members of the " Service " are carried on through a person who has no known connection with the Government. To his accomplices the Government agent is merely a man who has come to them with a profitable suggestion. They do not question his motives if his cash be good.

My connection with this delightful organisation necessitated a change of personality. I went round to the Quai d'Orsay and paid a few farewell calls to my friends there. I was going home, I said; and that afternoon the Grand Hotel lost one guest and " Le Lapin Agile " on the hill of Montmartre gained a new one. Acting under instructions I had become a social outcast myself.

The place where I had been told to stay had been a tavern for centuries. Once it was called the " Cabaret of the Assassins," then the " Cabaret of the Traitor," then " My Country Place," and now, after fifty years, it was " The Sprightly Rabbit." André Gill had painted the sign of the tavern, a rabbit, which hung in the street above the entrance. After I had taken

The Strong Arm Squad

my room—being careful to haggle long about the price, and finally securing a reduction of fifty centimes—for one does well to appear poor at "Le Lapin Agile"—I came down into the cabaret. It was crowded and the air was thick and warm with tobacco smoke. Disreputable couples were sitting around little wooden tables, drinking wretched wine from unlabelled bottles; an occasional shout arose for "tomatoes," a speciality of Frédéric, the proprietor, which was, in reality, a vile brew of absinthe and raspberry syrup. There was much shouting, and once or twice one of the company burst into song.

"Tomatoes," I told the waiter who came for my order. As he went I slipped a franc into his hand. "I want to see the Salmon. Is he in?"

He nodded.

A moment later a man stood before me. I saw a short, rather thick-set fellow, awkward but wiry, whose face bore somewhere the mark of a forgotten Irish ancestor. He was red-haired. I did not need his words to tell me who he was.

"I am the Salmon," he said. "What do you want?"

I studied him carefully before replying, appraising him as if he were a horse I contemplated buying. It was not tactful or altogether

The Strong Arm Squad

safe, as the Salmon's expression plainly showed; but I wished to be sure of my man. After a moment:

"Sit down, my friend. I have a business proposition to make. M. Morel sent me to you."

He smiled at the name. The fictitious M. Morel had put him in the way of several excellent " business propositions."

"It is a pleasure," responded the Salmon. "What does Monsieur wish?"

I told him.

In order to make you understand my business it is necessary that I should pause here, abandoning the Salmon for the moment, and recall to your memory a few facts about the political situation as it existed in this month of February, 1911. Europe at the time was lulled—to outward seeming. As everybody knows now, the forces that later brought about the War were then merrily at work, as indeed they had been for many years. But outwardly, save for the ever-impending certainty of trouble in the Balkans, the world of Europe was at peace.

But in America a storm was brewing. Mexico, which for so many years had been held at peace under the iron dictatorship of Diaz, was begin-

The Strong Arm Squad

ning to develop symptoms of organised discontent. Madero had taken the field, and although no one at the time believed in the ultimate success of the rebellion, it was evident that many changes might take place in the country, which would seriously affect the interests of thousands of European investors in Mexican enterprises. Consequently Europe was interested.

I do not purpose here to go into the events of those last days of Diaz's rule. That story has already been told many times and from various angles. I am merely interested in the European aspects of the matter, and particularly in the attitude of Germany.

Europe was interested, as I have said. Diaz was growing old and could certainly not last much longer. Then change must come. Was the Golden Age of the foreign investor, which had so long continued in Mexico, to continue still longer? Or would it end with the death of the Dictator?

To these questions, which were having their due share of attention in the chancelleries as well as in the commercial houses of Europe, came another, less apparent but more troublesome and more insistent than any of these. Japan, it was rumoured, although very faintly, was seeking to

The Strong Arm Squad

add to its considerable interest in Mexico by securing a strip of territory on the western coast of that country—an attempt which, if successful, would almost certainly bring about intervention by the United States.

My Government was especially interested in this movement on the part of Japan. It knew considerably more about the plan than any save the principals, for, as I happened to learn later, it had carefully encouraged the whole idea—for its own purposes. And it knew that at that very time the Financial Minister of Mexico, José Yves Limantour, was conducting preliminary negotiations in Paris with representatives of Japan, regarding the terms of a possible treaty. It knew that even then a protocol of this treaty was being drawn up.

There was only one thing that my Government wanted—a copy of the protocol. It was that which I had been instructed to get!

The personality of Limantour is one of the most interesting of our day. Brilliant, incorruptible, unquestionably the most able Mexican of his generation, he had for seventeen years been closely associated with the Dictator, and for a considerable portion of that period had been second only to Diaz in actual power. His presence

The Strong Arm Squad

in Paris at this time was significant. He had left Mexico on the 11th of July, 1910, ostensibly because of the poor health of his wife, although it had been reported that a serious break had taken place between himself and Diaz. He had spent a certain time in Switzerland, and had later come to Paris to arrange a loan of more than $100,000,000 with a group of English, French and German bankers. But this task had been completed in the early part of December, and in view of the unsettled conditions in Mexico there was no good reason for his continuing in Paris, save one—the negotiations with Japan.

It was this man against whom I was to fight —this man who had proved himself more than a match for some of the best brains of both hemispheres. The prospect was not reassuring. I knew that already several attempts had been made by our agents to secure the protocol, with the result that Limantour was sure to be more on his guard than he ordinarily would have been. Yet I *must* succeed—and it was plain that I could do so only by violence.

Violence it should be, then; and with the assistance of my friend the Salmon—to whom, you may be sure, I did not confide my real object—I prepared a plan of campaign, which we

The Strong Arm Squad

duly presented to a group of the Salmon's friends, who had been selected to assist us. To these men—Apaches, every one of them—I was presented as a decayed gentleman who for reasons of his own had found it necessary to join the forces of the Salmon. I was a good fellow, the Salmon assured them, and by way of proving my friendship I had shared with him my knowledge of a good "prospect" I had discovered.

"The man," I said, "always carries lots of money and jewellery." Of course, I did not tell them his name was Limantour. I said he always played cards late at his club. 'To stick him up," I said, "will be the simplest thing in the world, but we must be careful not to hurt him badly—not enough to set the police hot on our trail."

The Apaches fell in with the proposal enthusiastically. We would attempt it the following night.

Now the instructions which came to me under the sweat band of the black derby in the Café Américaine informed me that every night quite late Limantour received at his club a copy of the report of the day's conference with the Japanese envoy. It was prepared and delivered to Limantour by his secretary and it was his

The Strong Arm Squad

habit to study it, upon returning home, and plan out his line of attack for the negotiations of the following day. I concluded that Limantour therefore would have it (the report) on his person when he left the club.

Accordingly I had my Apaches waiting in the shadows. There were five of us. Limantour started to walk home, as I knew he was frequently in the habit of doing. We followed, and in the first quiet street that he ventured down he was felled. In his pockets we found a little money and some papers, one glance at which satisfied me that they were of no value.

My carefully-planned *coup* had failed. You can imagine how I felt about such a fiasco and how very quickly I had to think. Here was my first big chance and I had thoroughly and hopelessly bungled it! Limantour was already stirring. The blow he had received had purposely been made light. If he recovered to find himself robbed merely of an insignificant sum of money and some papers his suspicions would be aroused. I could not hope for another chance at him. I knew that Limantour was too clever not to sense something other than ordinary robbery in such an attack upon him. Furthermore, my Apaches had to be bluffed and deceived as thoroughly as

The Strong Arm Squad

he must be. I had promised them a victim who had loads of money, and at the few coins they had obtained there was much growling. Luckily I had a flash of sense. I resolved to turn the mishap to my advantage.

"We hit the wrong night, that's all," I muttered. "You take the coins and get away. I am going to try to fool him."

Like rats they scurried away. When Limantour came to, he found a very solicitous young man concerned about his welfare.

"I saw them from down the street," I told him. "They evidently knocked you out, but they cleared off when I came. Did they get anything from you? Here seem to be some letters." And from the pavement I picked up and restored to him the papers I had taken from his pocket not two minutes before.

Limantour accepted them and I knew that my audacity had triumphed.

"They are not of very much importance," said Limantour, "and I had only a few francs on me."

Then suddenly, as if he just realised that he was alive and unharmed, José Limantour began to thank me for my assistance. I thought of those who had told me he was a cold, hard, dis-

The Strong Arm Squad

tant man. Limantour flung his arms around my neck. I was his saviour! I was a very brave young gentleman! If I had not come up so boldly and promptly to his aid he might have been very badly beaten, perhaps even killed. For all he knew he owed me his life. He must thank me. He must know his preserver. Here was his card. Might he have mine? I had been wise enough to keep some of my old cards when I changed the rest of my personality from the Grand Hotel to Montmartre. I gave him one of them.

"A German!" he exclaimed, "and a worthy representative of that worthy race!" Limantour was enchanted. "And you live at the Grand Hotel?"

That was better still. I was only a sojourner in Paris and one might venture to offer me hospitality—no? Next day he would send round a formal invitation to come and dine at his house and meet his family. They would be delighted to meet this brave and intrepid hero and would also wish to thank me.

In an adjoining café we had a drink and parted for the night. Next morning of course I had to appear again at the Grand Hotel. On foot I walked away from "Le Lapin Agile," jumping

The Strong Arm Squad

into a taxi when I was out of sight. The taxi took me to the Gare du Nord; there I doubled on my tracks and presently, as if just having left a train, I took another taxi and was driven with my luggage to the hotel. I dropped around that afternoon to the Quai d'Orsay and called upon some of my acquaintances, remarking that I had changed my plans and would stay in Paris a little longer. That night I had the pleasure of dining with Limantour.

Thereafter I had to lead a double life. By day I was an habitué of prominent hotels, restaurants and clubs. I associated with young diplomats, and occasionally took a pretty girl to tea. By night I lived in " Le Lapin Agile " and consorted with thugs and their ilk. It cost me sleep, but I did not begrudge that in view of the stakes. All this time I was cultivating the acquaintance of Limantour and those around him.

Shortly afterwards I succeeded in taking one of the members of his household on a rather wild party, and when his head was full of champagne he blabbed that Limantour and his family were planning to sail for Cuba and Mexico on the following Saturday. I was also informed that on Friday, the day before the sailing, there would

The Strong Arm Squad

be a farewell reception at one of the embassies. Knowing Limantour's habits of work as I did by this time, I was able to lay my plans with as much certainty as prevails in my profession.

After weighing all the possibilities I decided to defer my attempt on him until this last Friday night. I reasoned that he would probably receive a draft of the agreement from his secretary at the club late that night. He would take it home with him and go over it with microscopic care. The next forenoon—Saturday—he would meet the Japanese envoy just long enough to finish the matter, and then he would hurry to the boat-train.

Of course, Limantour might act in a different way. That is the chance one has to take.

Friday night came. In his luxurious limousine Limantour and his family went to the farewell reception at the Embassy. Comparatively early he said his farewell—leaving Madame to go home later—and in his car he proceeded to the club. I saw him pass through the vestibule after leaving his chauffeur with instructions to wait. My guess as to Limantour's movements had been right, so the plans I had made worked smoothly.

I, too, had an automobile waiting near his

The Strong Arm Squad

club. Two of my men sauntered over to Limantour's car. Under pretence of sociability they invited his chauffeur to have a drink. They led him into a little café on a side street near by, the proprietor of which was in with the gang. Limantour's chauffeur had one drink and went to sleep. My men stripped him of his livery, which one of them donned. Presently Limantour had a new chauffeur sitting at the wheel of his limousine.

An hour later Limantour was seen hurrying out of the club. As a man will, he scarcely noticed his chauffeur, but cast a brief "Home!" to the man at the wheel. His limousine started, following a route through deserted residential streets, in one of which I had the trap ready. Half blocking the road was a large motor-car, apparently broken down. It was the automobile in which I had been waiting outside the club. In it were four of my Apaches. Limantour's car was called upon to stop.

"Can you lend me a wrench?" one of my men shouted to Limantour's false chauffeur.

His limousine stopped. That freemasonry which existed in the early days between motorists lent itself nicely to the situation. It was most natural for the chauffeur of Limantour's car to

GENERAL RAUL MADERO. (See p. 139)

GENERAL VILLA AND COLONEL TRINIDAD RODRIGUEZ.
See p. 120)

The Strong Arm Squad

get out and help my stalled motor. Indeed, Limantour himself opened the door of the limousine and, half protruding his body, called out with the kindest intentions.

To throw a chloroform-soaked towel over his head was the work of an instant. In half a minute he was having dreams—which I trust were pleasant. It was still necessary to keep my own men in the dark, to give these thugs no inkling that this was a diplomatic job. This time I was prepared, for I had learned of Limantour's habits in regard to carrying money on his person. In my right-hand overcoat pocket there were gold coins and bank-notes. With the leader of the gang I went through Limantour's clothes. In the darkness of that street it was a simple matter to seem to extract from them a double fistful of gold pieces and currency, which I turned over to the Salmon.

"Perhaps he has more bank-notes," I muttered, and I reached for the inner pocket of his coat. There my fingers closed upon a stiff document that made them tingle. "I'll just grab everything and we can go over it afterwards." Out of Limantour's possession into mine came pocket-book, letters, card-case and that heavy, familiar paper.

The Strong Arm Squad

Dumping the unconscious Limantour into his limousine, we cranked up our car and were off, leaving behind us at the worst plain evidence of a crime common enough in Paris. It was to be corroborated next morning by the discovery of a drunken chauffeur, for we took pains to go back and get him once more into his uniform and full of absinthe.

But it did not come to even that much scandal. Limantour, for obvious reasons, did not report the incident to the police. Next morning it was given out that Limantour had gone into the country and would not sail for a week. He had had a sudden recrudescence of an old throat trouble, and must rest and undergo treatment before undertaking the voyage to Mexico—so the specialist said. This report appeared in the Paris newspapers of the day. Of the protocol nothing was said at that time or later—by Señor Limantour.

I turned it over to the proper authorities in Berlin, and very soon departed from Montmartre, leaving behind me a well-contented group of Apaches, who assured me warmly that I was born for their profession. I did not argue the question with them.

There the matter might have ended; but Germany had another card to play. On February 27,

The Strong Arm Squad

1911, Limantour left Paris for New York, to confer with members of the Madero family, in order if possible to effect a reconciliation and to end the Madero revolt. He landed in New York on March 7. On that very day, by an odd coincidence, as one commentator* calls it, the United States mobilised 20,000 troops on the Mexican border!

It was no coincidence. The Wilhelmstrasse had read the proposed terms of the treaty with great interest. It had noted the secret clauses which gave Japan the lease of a coaling station, together with manœuvre privileges in Magdalena Bay, or at some other port on the Mexican coast which the Japanese Government might prefer. It had noted, too, that agreement which, although not expressly stipulating that Japan and Mexico should form an offensive and defensive alliance, implied that Japan would see to it that Mexico was protected against aggression.

And then Germany—acting always for her own interests—forwarded the treaty to Mexico, where it was placed in the hands of the American Ambassador, Henry Lane Wilson.

Mr. Wilson immediately left for Washington

* Mr. Edward I. Bell in "The Political Shame of Mexico."

The Strong Arm Squad

with a photograph of portions of the treaty. A Cabinet meeting was held. That night orders were sent out for the mobilisation of American troops, the assembling of United States marines in Guantanamo and the patrolling of the west coast of Mexico by warships of the United States.

Within a week Mr. Wilson had an interview in New York with Señor Limantour. Limantour left hurriedly for Mexico City, arriving there March 20. Conferences were held. Japan denied the existence of the treaty, and Washington recalled its war vessels and demobilised its troops. But barely seven weeks after Limantour arrived in Mexico, Madero, the bankrupt, with his handful of troops " captured " Ciudad Juarez. And shortly afterwards, Diaz, discredited and powerless, resigned the office he had held for a generation.

That is the story of the fall of Diaz so far as Germany was concerned in it. There were other elements involved, of course—but this is not a history of Mexico.

Germany had done the United States a service. It is interesting to consider the motives for her action. These motives may be explained in two words: South America.

The Strong Arm Squad

Germany, let it be understood, wants South America, and has wanted it for many years. Not as a possession—the Wilhelmstrasse is not insane —but as a customer and an ally. Like many other nations, Germany has seen in the countries of Latin America an invaluable market for her own goods and an unequalled producer of raw supplies for her own manufacturers. She has sought to control that market to the best of her abilities. But she has also done what no other European nation has dared to do—she has attempted to form alliances with the South American countries which, in the event of war between the United States and Germany, would create a diversion in Germany's favour, and effectively tie the hands of the United States so far as any offensive action was concerned.

There was just one stumbling-block to this plan: the Monroe Doctrine. It was patent to German diplomats that such an alliance could never be secured unless the South American countries were roused to such a degree of hostility against the United States that they would welcome an opportunity to affront the Government which had proclaimed that Doctrine. And Germany, casting about for a means of making trouble, had encouraged the Japanese-Mexican

The Strong Arm Squad

alliance, hoping for intervention in Mexico and the subsequent arousal of fear and ill-feeling towards the United States on the part of the South American countries.

And Germany had been so anxious for the United States to intervene in Mexico that she had not only encouraged a treaty which would be inimical to American interests, but had made certain that knowledge of this treaty should come into the United States Government's hands by placing it there herself!

The United States did not intervene and Germany for the moment failed. But Germany did not give up hope. The intrigue against the United States through Mexico had only begun.

It has not ended yet.

CHAPTER VI

A HERO IN SPITE OF MYSELF

My letter again—I go to America and become a United States soldier—Sent to Mexico and sentenced to death there — I join Villa's army and gain an undeserved reputation.

I MUST leave Europe behind me now and go on to the period embraced in the last five years. A private soldier in the United States Army; the victim of an attempt at assassination in stormy Mexico; major in the Mexican army; once again German secret agent and aide of Franz von Papen, the German Military Attaché in Washington; prisoner under suspicion of espionage in a British prison, and finally the American Government's central witness in the summer of 1916, in a case that was the sensation of its hour—these are the rôles I have been called on to play in that brief space of time.

In the month of April, 1912, I abruptly quitted the service of my Government. The reasons which impelled me were very serious. You remember that my active life began with the dis-

A Hero in Spite of Myself

covery of a document of such personal and political significance that Government agents followed me all over Europe until I drove a bargain with them for it. In the winter of 1912, by a chain of circumstances I must keep to myself, that self-same document came again into my possession. I knew enough then, and was ambitious enough, to determine that this time I would utilise to the full the power which possession of it gave me. But it could not be used in Germany. Therefore I disappeared.

There was an immediate search for me, which was most active in Russia. I was not in Russia nor in Europe. After running over in mind all the most unlikely places where I could lose myself I had found one that seemed ideal.

While they were scouring Russia for me I was making my way across the Atlantic Ocean in the capacity of steward in the steerage of the steamship *Kroonland* of the Red Star Line.

The *Kroonland* docked in New York City in May, 1912. I left her as abruptly as I had left a prouder service. Three days later, a sorry-looking vagabond, I had applied for enlistment in the United States Army and had been accepted. I was sent to the recruiting camp at

A Hero in Spite of Myself

Fort Slocum, and under the severe eye of a sergeant began to learn my drill.

It was towards the middle of May that I—or rather, "Frank Wachendorf"—enlisted. After a stretch of recruit-training at Fort Slocum I was assigned to the Nineteenth Infantry, then at Fort Leavenworth, Kansas.

I learned my drill—shades of Gross Lichterfelde!—with extreme ease. That is the only single thing that I was officially asked to do.

But early in my short and pleasant career as a United States soldier something happened which gave me special occupation. My small library was discovered. Among the volumes were Mahan's "Sea Power" and Gibbon's "Decline and Fall" —not just the books one would look for among the possessions of a country lout hardly able to stammer twenty words in English. But the mishap turned in my favour. My captain sent for me.

"Wachendorf," he said, "you probably have your own reasons for being where you are. That is none of my business. But you don't have to stay there. If you want to go in for a commission you are welcome to my books and to any aid I can give you."

Thereafter life in the Nineteenth was decidedly

A Hero in Spite of Myself

agreeable. I set myself sincerely and wholeheartedly the task of winning a commission in the United States Army. I believe I might eventually have won it, too. But Fate revealed other plans for me when I had been an American soldier some nine months.

That winter of 1913, you remember, had been a stormy period in Mexico. Huerta had made his *coup d'état*. Francisco Madero had been deposed and murdered. President Taft had again mobilised part of the United States forces on the border, leaving his successor, President Wilson, to deal with a Southern neighbour in the throes of revolution.

The Nineteenth Infantry was ordered to Galveston, Texas. And in Galveston the agents of Berlin suddenly put their fingers on me again. It happened in the Public Library. I was reading a book there one day when a man I knew well came and sat down beside me. We will call him La Vallée—born and bred a Frenchman, but one of Germany's most trusted agents.

"*Wie geht's, von der Goltz?*" was his greeting.

I told him he had mistaken me for someone else. He laughed.

"What's the use of bluffing?" he asked, "when each of us knows the other? Just read

A Hero in Spite of Myself

these instructions I'm carrying." He laid a paper before me.

La Vallée's instructions were brief and outwardly not threatening. Find von der Goltz, they bade him. Try to make him realise how great a wrong he was guilty of when he deserted his country. But let him understand, too, that his Government appreciates his services and believes he acted impulsively. If he will prove his loyalty by returning to his duty his mistake will be blotted out.

I read carefully and asked La Vallée how I was expected to prove my loyalty at that particular time.

"You know what it is like in Mexico now," he said. "Our Government has heavy interests there. Your services are needed in helping to look out for them."

"But," I objected, "I am a soldier in the United States Army. You are asking me to be a deserter."

"Germany," said La Vallée, "has the first claim on every German. If your duty happens to make you seem a deserter, that is all right. Frank Wachendorf must manage to bear the disgrace. Speaking of that," he added, carelessly enough, but eyeing me severely, "were you not

A Hero in Spite of Myself

indiscreet there? Suppose some enemy should find out that you made false statements when you enlisted? I believe there is a penalty."

La Vallée knew that he had me in his power. I had to yield, and was told to report to the German Consul at Juarez, across the Rio Grande from El Paso. So in March, 1918, Frank Robert Wachendorf, private, became a deserter from the United States Army and a reward of $50 was offered for his arrest.

Before I crossed the border I had one very important piece of business to attend to, and I stopped in El Paso long enough to finish it. Mexico, under the conditions that prevailed, was an ideal trap for me. As the lesser of two evils I had decided to risk my body there. But I had no mind to risk also what was to Berlin of far more value than my body—namely, that document which, a year before, had led to my abrupt departure from Germany and her service.

In El Paso, where I was utterly unacquainted, I had to find some friend in whose stanchness I could put the ultimate trust. Being a Roman Catholic, I made friends with a priest and led him into gossip about different members of his flock. He spoke of a harnessmaker and saddler, one E. Koglmeier, an unmarried man of about

A Hero in Spite of Myself

fifty, who kept a shop in South Santa Fe Street. He was, the priest said, the most simple-minded, simple-hearted and utterly faithful man he knew.

I lost no time in making Koglmeier's acquaintance, on the priest's introduction, and we soon were on friendly terms. When I crossed the international bridge I left behind in his safe a sealed package of papers. He knew only that he was to speak to no one about them and was to deliver them only to me in person or to a man who bore my written order for them.

I reported to the German Consul in Juarez. He asked me to carry on to Chihuahua certain reports and letters addressed to Kueck, the German Consul there. From Chihuahua Kueck sent me on to Parral with other documents. And a German official in Parral gave me another parcel of papers to carry back to Kueck.

I had no sooner reached Chihuahua on the return trip than I was put under arrest by an officer of the Federal (Huertista) forces, then in control of the city. I asked on whose authority. On that, he said, of General Salvador Mercado. I was a spy engaged in disseminating anti-Federal propaganda. I had to laugh at the sheer absurdity of that, and asked what proofs he had to sustain such charges.

A Hero in Spite of Myself

"The papers you are carrying," he said then, "will be proof enough, I think."

Chihuahua was under martial law. I had not the slightest inkling as to what might be in those papers I had so obligingly transported. I had put my foot into it, as the saying goes, up to my neck, the place where a noose fits.

They marched me up to the barracks and into the presence of General Mercado. That was June 23, 1913, at 9 o'clock in the evening.

General Salvador Mercado, then the supreme authority in Chihuahua, with practical powers of life and death over its people, proved to be a squat, thick, bull-necked man with the face of an Indian and the bearing of a bully.

His first words stirred my temper to the bottom, luckily for me. If I had confronted the man with any other emotion than raging anger I should not be alive now.

"Your Consul will do no good," he told me sneeringly. "He says you are not a German. You are a Gringo. You are a bandit and a robber. You have turned spy against us too. I am going to make short work of you. But first you are going to tell me all you know."

As the completeness of the charge flashed upon me I went wild. There was a chair beside

A Hero in Spite of Myself

me. I converted one leg into a club and started for Mercado. The five other men in the room got the best hold upon me that they could. By the time they had mastered me Mercado had backed away into the farthest corner of the room.

The remainder of our interview was stormy and fruitless. It resulted in my being taken to Chihuahua penitentiary, the strongest prison in Mexico, and thrown into a cell. It was two months and a half before I came out again.

There is small use going in detail into the major and minor degradations of life in a Mexican prison. I pass over *cimex lectularius* and the warfare which ended with my release. There are more edifying things to tell. For instance, how I came into possession of half a blanket and a pair of friends.

I was confined—a sentry with fixed bayonet standing before my door—in an upper tier in the officers' wing. Usually confinement in the officers' wing carried one special privilege in which I, the desperado, did not share. During the day the cell doors were left open and the prisoners had the run of the corridor and galleries. My sentry's bayonet barred them from me, but could not keep them from talking of the new prisoner who claimed to be a German and was

A Hero in Spite of Myself

suffering because he was suspected of attachment to the Constitutionalist cause.

On my third or fourth night there I was attracted to my cell door by a sibilant "Oiga, Alemán!" and something soft was thrust between the bars.

"German," whispered a voice in Spanish out of the blackness, "it is cold to-night. We have brought you up a blanket."

So began my friendship with Pablo Almandaris and Rafael Castro, two young Constitutionalist officers. Almandaris, in particular, later became a chum of mine. He was a long, lank, solemn individual, the very image of Don Quixote of La Mancha. I remember him with love, because he was the man who gave to me in prison, out of kindness of heart, a full half of his single blanket.

This is how it happened. He and Rafael Castro, who were cell-mates, had contrived a way to pick their lock and roam the cell block at night, stark naked, their brown skins blending perfectly with the dingy walls. They had already heard the story of my plight. That night Almandaris had cut his blanket in two, and the pair, with the bit of wool and a bottle of tequilla they had bought that day when the prison market was

CAPTAIN VON DER GOLTZ'S COMMISSION AS MAJOR IN THE MEXICAN CONSTITUTIONALIST ARMY. (*See p.* 139)

A Hero in Spite of Myself

open, sneaked up to the gallery and my cell. They gave the liquor to the sentry, who, being an Indian, promptly drank the whole of it down and became blissfully unconscious.

The blanket was the first of many gifts, and many were the chats we had together, all with a practical purpose.

"If you ever escape or are released," Almandaris kept telling me, "go to Trinidad Rodriguez. He is my colonel. And if you ever get out of Mexico go to El Paso and hunt up Labansat. He is there."

So they contrived to alleviate the minor evils of my predicament, and I shall never forget them. The major difficulty was beyond their reach. The trap had closed completely round me. The charge of spying and Mercado's general truculence were only cloaks for a more subtle hostility from another quarter. The reason for my imprisonment was soon revealed openly.

I had made various attempts to communicate with Kueck, the German Consul. Always I met the retort that Kueck himself said I was no German. At the same time, managing to smuggle an appeal for aid to the American Consul, I was informed that etiquette forbade his taking any steps on my behalf. Kueck himself,

A Hero in Spite of Myself

he said, had told him the German Consulate was doing all it could to protect me. It did not need a Bismarck to grasp the implications of those contradictory statements.

After I had been in prison for about three weeks Kueck came to see me and made the whole matter thoroughly plain.

"Von der Goltz," he opened bluntly, "you are in a bad situation."

"Do you think so?" I asked him significantly.

"I have every reason to think so," he said. "My hands are tied. I positively can take no steps in your behalf, unless "—he looked straight at me—"unless you restore certain documents you have no right to possess."

They had me nicely. The surrender of my letter was the price I must pay for my life. Acting under instructions, he had made me a definite offer. I had to take it or leave it.

I could not give the letter up. It was my guarantee of safety. As long as Kueck did not know where it was I was valuable to him only while alive. Furthermore, I had some hopes of being freed by outside aid. Through Almandaris I had learned that the Constitutionalists were attacking Chihuahua, with good hope of taking the city. I knew that if they succeeded, the

A Hero in Spite of Myself

German—whose suffering for their cause, I was told, was known throughout their forces—would be well cared for. So I reached my decision.

"Herr Consul," I said, "I will not give up the papers you refer to. I am not a child. Those papers are in a safe place. So are instructions as to their disposal in case of emergency. Let anything happen to me, and within a fortnight every newspaper in the United States will be printing the most sensational story within memory."

On July 23, 1913, I was tried by court-martial and sentenced to death. That led to a bitter personal quarrel between General Manuel Chao, the Constitutionalist commander attacking the city, and Mercado, who defended it.

Chao sent in a flag of truce, absolving me from any connection with his cause and threatening that, if I were killed, Mercado personally would have to pay the score when the Constitutionalists took Chihuahua. The Indian bully retorted that if the Constitutionalists ever captured the city they would not find their pet alive there.

Three times in the weeks that followed the Constitutionalist forces seemed on the point of capturing Chihuahua. Have you ever walked out with your own firing squad and spent an endless half hour on a chilly morning in the company

A Hero in Spite of Myself

of an officer with drawn sword, five soldiers with loaded rifles and a sergeant with the revolver destined to give you your *coup de grâce?* Three times that happened to me, at Mercado's orders! My profession has seldom permitted me to indulge in personal hatreds, but as I was marched back from that third bad half-hour my mind was filled with one thought: If ever I got Mercado where he had me then I would let him know what it felt like.

Then matters came to a crisis. Reinforcements were brought up from Mexico City and the Constitutionalist besiegers suffered a crushing defeat. I could put no more hope in them.

Kueck came again to see me.

"Give me an order on Koglmeier for those papers," he demanded. "There's no use saying Koglmeier hasn't got them, for I know he has."

I could see he was not bluffing, and knew the game was up. I signed the release for the papers. There had been no personal animosity between Kueck and myself. I had seen too much of life to be angry with a man simply because he was obeying his orders.

About September 12, 1913, Kueck came to escort me out of prison, and in his own carriage drove me to the railway station, bound north, out

A Hero in Spite of Myself

of Mexico. I had a sheaf of letters, signed by Kueck, which recommended me, as Baron von der Goltz, to the good offices of German Consular representatives throughout the United States, and requested them to supply me with funds.

The last man who spoke to me in Chihuahua was Colonel Carlos Orozco, commander of the Sixth Battalion of Infantry, and General Mercado's right-hand man, though his bitter enemy. His farewell was a threat. "You are lucky to get out of Mexico," he told me. "If you ever come back and I see you I will have you shot at once." My next meeting with Colonel Carlos Orozco occurred on Mexican soil.

Escorted by Consul Kueck out of Mexico I went up to El Paso, determined to return to Mexico as soon as possible. But before I did anything else I felt a very great desire to square accounts with General Salvador Mercado.

So I stepped off at El Paso to look for Labansat, the Constitutionalist about whom my friend Pablo Almandaris told me while I was in prison. I lost no time in getting into touch with him and other members of the Constitutionalist junta.

Another acquaintance made at that time proved very useful to me later. Dr. L. A.

A Hero in Spite of Myself

Rachbaum, Francisco Villa's personal physician, was a fellow guest at the Ollendorf Hotel.

We were an earnest but impecunious bunch. Juan T. Burns, afterwards Mexican Consul-General in New York, may recall a morning when he and I found ourselves with one nickel between us and the necessity of getting breakfast for two at an El Paso lunch counter. That lone "jitney" bought a cup of coffee and two rolls. Each of us took a roll and we drank the cup of coffee mutually.

I also renewed my intimacy with Koglmeier, the saddler in South Santa Fe Street. He told me a man he did not know had come with my written order for the papers I had left in his safe and he had given them up.

Despairing at last of obtaining results at El Paso, I availed myself of my consular recommendations and went on to Los Angeles, California. There I received help from Geraldine Farrar, whom I had known in Germany, and in November, 1913, directly after the battle of Tierra Blanca, Chihuahua, I received a telegram saying: "Dr. Rachbaum proposition accepted; come with the next train," and signed "General Villa." My way lay open before me and I was free to start.

A Hero in Spite of Myself

I reached El Paso on November 27 and went on to Chihuahua, which had fallen into the hands of the Constitutionalists. Once there, I looked up my friend of the half blanket, Pablo Almandaris, and by him was introduced to Colonel Trinidad Rodriguez, commanding a cavalry brigade, who promptly attached me to his staff, with the rank of captain.

The Federalists had retreated across the desert northwards and settled themselves in Ojinaga, the so-called Gibraltar of the Rio Grande, a tremendously strong natural position.

Towards the middle of December we received orders to proceed to the attack of Ojinaga. Our brigade and the troops of Generals Panfilo Natira and Toribio Ortega were included in the expedition, some 7,000 men. The railway carried us seventy miles. The rest of the journey had to be made on horseback. During four days of marching in the desert I made acquaintance with Mexican mounted infantry, the most effective arm for such conditions and country the world has seen.

Arriving before the outer defences of Ojinaga we began our siege of the city. Soon afterwards, I got my first sight of Pancho Villa.

Of a sudden, one evening, Trinidad Rodriguez

A Hero in Spite of Myself

told me that "Pancho" had just arrived, and we must ride over for a conference with him.

We found Villa lying on a saddle blanket in an irrigation ditch in the company of Raul Madero, brother of the murdered President, a handful of officers who had come up with them, and our own commanders, Natira and Ortega.

Madero, to my mind one of the ablest Mexicans alive, was clad in the dingiest of old grey sweaters. Villa, unkempt, unshaven and unshorn, was begrimed and weary from his ride across the desert. But he seemed full of bottled-up energy, and when General Rodriguez and I came up he was giving General Ortega a talking to because so little had been accomplished in regard to the taking of Ojinaga.

While we talked I fashioned a cigarette, and all at once he broke off abruptly. "Give me some of that too," he demanded. I handed him "the makings," and he attempted a cigarette. He was so clumsy with it that I had to roll it for him. Then for the first and last time in my acquaintance with him I saw Pancho Villa smoke. Contrary to the stories that have gone out about him, he is a most abstemious man with regard to alcohol and tobacco.

On Christmas night, 1913, happened the ad-

A Hero in Spite of Myself

venture which made me, quite by accident, and without intention, a hero. Also, I underwent the greatest fright of my life.

My commander, Rodriguez, had received orders to make an attack that night straightforward towards Ojinaga. After it was completely dark we formed and advanced, finding ourselves very soon among the willows lining the bank of the Rio Conchos, which we had to cross.

It was my first taste of genuine warfare, and I cannot begin to tell you how it affected me, how ghastly it was among the willows in the vague darkness through which the column was threading its way with the utmost possible quietness. The beat of hoofs was muffled in the soggy ground, and the only sound to break the utter stillness of the night was the occasional clank of a spur or thin neigh of a horse.

Then all at once, to the front and in the distance, came a boom—the single growling of a field-gun. Ping! Ping! Ping! broke out a volley of rifle shots, and then with its r-r-r-r-r! a Hotchkiss machine-gun got to work. A staccato bam! bam! bam! as a Colt's machine-gun joined the chorus. Somewhere troops were going into serious action. That was no skirmishing.

A Hero in Spite of Myself

We finally crossed the river and dismounted. Part of the brigade had gone astray. Rodriguez cursed impatiently and incessantly under his breath until he joined us. He was a born cavalry leader, mad for action. Any sort of waiting lacerated his nerves.

In line, with rifles trailing, we moved across the unknown terrain of low, rolling hills. On our front there had been no firing. Then all at once, directly before us and not far ahead, sounded a startled "Quí vive?" and an instant's silence while the surprised outpost of the enemy waited for an answer. "Alerta! Alerta!" sounded his shrill alarm.

Hell broke open around us then. Rifles, machine-guns and cannon opened fire all at once. Bullets whined above our heads and bursting shrapnel fell around us. We had just come to an irrigation ditch, six feet wide, with a high wire fence on the farther bank of it.

"Stay here till they're all across and look for skulkers!" Trinidad Rodriguez gave himself time to order me, then leaped across the ditch and began to run towards the fence. "Come on here, boys!" he shouted.

The men were quickly across. I followed, or tried to, and just as my front foot touched the

A Hero in Spite of Myself

farther bank the clay crumbled. Down I went into the ditch.

When I recovered myself in that four feet of mud and water and poked my head up over the bank the fence had been demolished. Beyond it countless rifles spat tongues of fire towards me. But not a living soul was near. The night had swallowed up the very last one of our men.

Fright had not come yet. I was bewildered. I still had my rifle and began to use it. After a few discharges there came a violent wrench and the barrel parted company with the rest of the weapon. It had been shot to pieces in my hands. I threw the stock away and got out my revolver —a Colt .44 single-action, of the frontier model.

Boom! There was a roar like a field-gun's and a flash that lit up the night all round me. The wet weapon was outdoing itself in pyrotechnics, and I was unnecessarily attracting attention to myself. So, half swimming, half wading, I moved down the ditch in the direction of the high hill which, looming vaguely, seemed half familiar to me.

I was lost, you understand. I had come at night into unknown terrain. I welcomed that hill, which seemed to give me back my bearings.

A Hero in Spite of Myself

I reached the base of it, got out of my ditch and began to climb, with some caution, luckily for me. For just as I stole over the crest a roar and a flash obliterated the night. Two enemy fieldpieces had been discharged together, almost into my face.

Deeming it more than likely that the flash had shown the gunners one startled Teutonic face, I rolled down that hill and was once more in my ditch. But panic had full possession of me. I climbed out on the far side and ran among the scattered trees there until I realised that no racer can hope to outpace a bullet. Then I stopped.

Phut! Phut! Bullets were hissing into the soft irrigated ground all round me, for by accident I had gotten into a very dangerous zone of dropping cross-fire, while overhead shrapnel was searching out blindly for our horses.

By good luck I knew the trumpet calls. Whenever the signal to fire sounded I took what cover I could, going on again in what I decided was the direction of the Rio Conchos as soon as the bugles called "cease firing."

After a while I found a small grey horse standing dejectedly by a tree. I mounted him and eventually got among the willows on the river bank. There the horse collapsed under me

A Hero in Spite of Myself

without a warning quiver or groan, and when I had wriggled myself loose and groped him over I discovered the poor brute must have been shot as full of holes as a flute before I ever found him.

But I had small sympathy to spend on fallen horses just then. Cleaning my gory hands as best I could on breeches and tunic, I stumbled on through the bushes. After a long time I came, by accident, to the place where the brigade had dismounted to go into action. The mounts were mostly gone, but a few still stood there, with perhaps a score of men and one officer, Lieutenant-Colonel Patricio, who was vastly surprised at my sudden appearance from the direction of the front.

Our brigade had been withdrawn within twenty minutes of the beginning of the action—as soon as it was quite certain the surprise had failed. Patricio was waiting there because his brother had been killed, and he wanted, if possible, to take back his body.

"But," cried the colonel, suddenly warming into emotion, "you—where have you been? You, valiant German, refused to come back with the others! All night, all by yourself, you have been fighting single-handed. Let me embrace you!"

A Hero in Spite of Myself

He flung his arms about me, to receive a fresh surprise. "You are all sticky with something," he cried. "What is it?"

"Blood," I told him simply and truthfully. My reputation was made.

Bravado stirs a Mexican as nothing else can. Counterfeit bravado is just as effective as any so long as the substitution is not suspected. Young Captain von der Goltz, in his first real engagement, had got stupidly lost and very badly frightened. But of Captain von der Goltz Colonel Patricio and his troopers sang the praises for days thereafter to every officer and every peon soldier they met. He had fought on alone for hours after every comrade left him. He had bathed himself in the blood of his enemies, up to his hips and up to his shoulders. You could see it on his clothes.

By the time Ojinaga fell "El Diablo Alemán"—"the German devil"—had become a tradition of the Constitutionalist Army.

Ojinaga fell at New Year, 1914, the Federalists retreating across the Rio Grande into the United States. We pursued them. And on the bank of the river I had a little adventure.

You remember that when I left Chihuahua, a released prisoner, the last person who spoke to

A Hero in Spite of Myself

me was Colonel Carlos Orozco, commanding the Sixth Infantry Battalion, and his farewell was a threat (*see* p. 117).

That Sixth Battalion had been engaged in the defence of Ojinaga and had retreated with its fellow-organisations. When I came up to the Rio Grande a small body of fugitives was in midstream. My handful of troopers rode in, surrounded them and brought them back to Mexico. Their heroic commander, who had offered no show of resistance, proved to be Orozco, with the colours of his outfit wrapped round his body, under his blouse!

The provocation was too much for me. "Don Carlos," I asked him, "is it possible you have forgotten me? When we parted last time you promised to shoot me if ever we met again. I am naturally all on fire to learn whether you are thinking of keeping your promise now."

Prominent prisoners were getting short shrift in those days, and Orozco preserved a sullen silence. But I let him ford the river to safety. He eventually got back to Mexico City and Huerta, by way of San Antonio, Galveston and Vera Cruz. The story of his exploit at Ojinaga, the sole Federal officer to come out of it alive, unwounded, and bringing his colours with him,

A Hero in Spite of Myself

furnished columns of copy to *El Imparcial* and the other papers. Friends and admirers of his who heard the lion roar at that time may find some interest in this less romantic record of his adventure.

I had another account to settle with my old acquaintance, Consul Kueck of Chihuahua. During the last battle before Ojinaga an officer struck up a rifle which he saw a peon aiming at my back. The ball whistled over my head. The soldier later saw fit to confess the reason for his act. He said that a big, fat German—Kueck's secretary, he thought—had come to him just before we left Chihuahua on our expedition and had given him 500 pesos to attempt my life.

Returning to Chihuahua very soon after New Year's Day, I made it my business to call on Consul Kueck. He had cleared out across the border to El Paso just before we got in.

Failing the principal, I took the liberty of arresting Kueck's secretary inside the sacred precincts of the Foreign Club. After my adjutant and he and I had had three or four hours' private talk, and he understood how likely he was to occupy the cell in Chihuahua penitentiary which had once been mine, he helped me obtain copies of certain documents in the consular

BRIGADA TORIBIO ORTEGA
MAYORIA.
NUM

Por el presente hago constar que el portador Sr. Horst von der Goltz, ha militado bajo mis órdenes con el grado de Mayor de nuestro Ejército siendo actualmente miembro de mi Estado Mayor y por lo tanto me permito recomendarlo a las atenciones de los que el presente vieren por lo que anticipo las gracias.

Constitución y Reforma,
Chihuahua, Chih., 8-1-14.
El General,
Raul Madero

GENERAL RAUL MADERO'S LETTER OF RECOMMENDATION. (See p. 141)

BRIGADA TORIBIO ORTEGA
MAYORIA.
NUM

Este Cuartel General ha tenido a bien conceder a Ud la licencia que ha solicitado para separarse del servicio de esta Brigada por el término de seis meses pudiendo prorrogarse por más tiempo al ser solicitado por Ud

Constitución y Reforma
Chihuahua Chih. 8-1-14
El General,
Raul Madero

SIX MONTHS' LEAVE FROM GEN. RAUL MADERO GRANTED TO CAPTAIN VON DER GOLTZ. (See p. 141)

A Hero in Spite of Myself

archives, particularly the letter Kueck had written to the American Consul affirming himself to be fully responsible for my safety, at the very time when he was setting Mercado on and telling me that he could and would do nothing for me. Once I got hold of that I felt fairly certain that Kueck would be moderate in his dealings with me thereafter.

Only General Salvador Mercado stood wholly on the debit side of my account book. I had heard that he had been captured on United States soil, along with numerous other fugitive Federal officers, and been put for safe keeping into the detention camp at El Paso.

It chanced that Villa and Raul Madero went up to the border for a few days of the winter race-meet at Juarez, just across the river from El Paso. Don Raul was kind enough to invite me, too, and I went along in fettle, with a new uniform. Our army was in funds and I had all the money I wanted.

From Juarez it was merely a matter of crossing the international bridge to be in El Paso. I went over. I wanted to see Koglmeier, the saddler in South Santa Fe Street, and I wanted to visit the detention camp.

I chose to see the camp first, and had the

A Hero in Spite of Myself

forethought to fill one of the pockets of my overcoat with Mexican gold pieces, very welcome to my whilom enemies. Poor fellows, they were, most of them, in the tattered clothing they had worn when captured. Their faces were wan and meagre and they were glad enough to accept, along with my greeting, the bits of gold I contrived to slip into their hands.

In the centre of the camp we came upon a tent more imposing than its mates, though by no means palatial.

"This," said my cicerone, "is the quarters of General Mercado, the ranking officer here. Do you wish to pay him your respects?"

As I have said, Salvador Mercado is squat and thick in build, with a bull neck. Some day, I fear, he is going to die of apoplexy, if he does not fall, more gloriously, in action. He shows certain apoplectic symptoms. For instance, as we stepped inside his tent and he saw who one of his visitors was, his neck swelled till it threatened to burst his collar.

"My General," I assured him warmly, "it is indeed a pleasure and an honour to see you again. I trust the climate up here agrees with you?" I did not offer him a gold piece when he said good-bye.

A Hero in Spite of Myself

From the detention camp I went to Koglmeier's shop in South Santa Fe Street. Both front and rear doors were standing open, and through the back of one I could see Koglmeier's horse, a beast I had often ridden, switching its tail in the yard, which was its stable. I went into the store. "Koglmeier!" I called. "Oh, Koglmeier!"

From the side of the shop stepped out a man on whom I had never set eyes before.

"Koglmeier ain't here."

"But he must be here," I insisted. "I can see his horse out there in the yard."

"Yes," said the man, "the horse is here, but Koglmeier ain't. Nor he won't be. It just happens that Koglmeier's dead."

"When did he die?"

"The 20th of last December," said the man. "But he didn't die. He got murdered."

On the night of that 20th of December, Koglmeier, the quietest, most inoffensive man in El Paso, had been murdered in his shop. It looked, said my informant, "like his head had been beat in with a hatchet, or something." Robbery apparently had not been the motive, for his possessions were untouched. If he had made an outcry it had not attracted attention, perhaps

A Hero in Spite of Myself

because a carousal was going full blast in the vacant lot beside his place of business. The authorities were utterly at sea, and still are. The United States Department of Justice agents told me they could find no motive for the murder. I knew the motive. Koglmeier had kept "my documents" for me; therefore Imperial Germany had willed he should die.

Koglmeier was the only German in El Paso who was a friend of mine, and knew of the existence of those documents which I had been forced to give up through the agency of Mercado's firing squads.

His end subdued the festive spirit in me, and I was not sorry when we started back for the interior of Mexico.

Torreon was taken by Villa on April 2, 1914, and we settled down there for a brief period of rest and recuperation. Rest! Torreon stands out in my memory as the scene of the most hectic activity I have indulged in. Raul Madero and I have since laughed over the ludicrousness of it. But at the time it was deadly serious. My reputation was at stake. I managed to save it barely by the skin of its teeth.

Chief Trinidad Rodriguez got twenty machine-guns down from the United States and turned

A Hero in Spite of Myself

them over to me. "Train your gun crews and get the platoons ready for field service," he ordered. "You can have three weeks. Then I shall need them."

Without a word I saluted and turned on my heel. I could not very well tell my General that I had never in my life applied even the tip of one finger to a machine-gun.

The guns arrived next day, as promised. They had been sent to us bare, just the barrels and tripods. There were no holsters, no pack saddles for either guns or ammunition, not one of the accessories which equip a machine-gun company for action. I had to start from the ground, in literal truth. And I had not a soul to advise me how to begin.

We loaded the guns on to our wagons, took them over to camp, and laid them side by side in a long row down the centre of an empty warehouse in Torreon.

That satisfied me for one afternoon. I went over to General Rodriguez's quarters.

"I've got the guns," I reported.

"Good!" he cried. "I shall want the platoons ready for action in three weeks. Not a day later."

It was up to me to have them ready. So I got busy at once.

A Hero in Spite of Myself

My first move was an abduction. There happened to be in Torreon jail at that time a first-class bank robber named Jefferson, who was being held for the arrival of extradition papers from Texas. The day after my guns arrived Jefferson escaped, and though the authorities made diligent search they failed to find him. He knew more about machine-guns than I did. His profession had made him an excellent mechanic. Furthermore, he had Yankee ingenuity and American "git up and git." We soon had all twenty guns set up in working order.

Then came the problem of the gun crews. Our Indians, slow, thick-headed, stubborn and stolid, were no fit material for such highly specialised work. Machine-gun manipulation requires very peculiar qualifications in every man concerned. Three men compose the crew. One squats behind the shield and pulls the trigger. The second, prone, slides the clips of cartridges into the breach. The third passes up the supply of ammunition. At any moment the gun may heat and jam. Also at any moment any one of the trio may fall, yet his work must be carried on. I had seen a gunner sit on the dying body of a comrade and coolly aim and fire, the action being so hot there was not time to drag the wounded

A Hero in Spite of Myself

man aside. You cannot take an Indian wild from the hills and in twenty-one days fit him to do such work as that by any course of training.

My only resort was to get my gun crews ready made.

A brigade not far away from ours possessed machine-gun platoons which were the pride of its heart. I looked at them, and broke first the Tenth and then the Eighth Commandment.

To a wise old sergeant I gave a hundred pesos.

"Juan," I told him, "get the men of those machine-gun crews drunk in this quarter of Torreon. And encourage them to be noisy."

Juan obeyed instructions. Once the beer and mezcal took hold, the men I wanted became boisterous enough to justify our provost guard in running them all in. The rest was simple. The breach of discipline was condoned by General Rodriguez only on condition that the culprits were turned over to him for further discipline.

So I got my gun crews. I was beginning to have hopes. The best saddler in the city was making holsters. When I first approached him with an order he had promptly thrown up his hands. "There is not a scrap of leather left in Torreon," he said.

I instantly thought of chair backs. In Spanish

A Hero in Spite of Myself

countries furniture upholstered in old carved Cordovan leather is an heirloom. In time of war ruthlessness is a useful quality. I soon presented my saddler with sufficient leather for my purpose and could turn my attention to pack saddles. Not even the sawhorse frames were procurable in Torreon, but wood was plentiful. And there was a jail filled with idle prisoners. Ten days after the first sight of my guns I was able to report to General Rodriguez that the platoons were coming along.

"But I have no mules for them yet," I hinted.

He sent a hundred next day, beauties, fat, strong, in the pink of condition. But they had come straight down from the tableland. They could be trusted to kick saddles, guns, tripods, holsters and ammunition cases into nothing at the least provocation.

Torreon was celebrating its new Constitutionalism with daily bull fights. Each afternoon, while the fight was on, the plaza before the entrance to the ring was crowded with public rigs in waiting, all drawn by sorry-looking mules, half fed and too worn out to have a single kick left in them.

With a squad of troopers I descended on the plaza one day. No cabby anywhere is markedly

A Hero in Spite of Myself

shy or retiring, and these were hill-bred muleteers. But we got the mules in the end.

"You are getting the best of the bargain," I assured them. "I am only swopping with you. In the corral I have a hundred fine, strong, new mules worth three times as much as these played-out beasts you are getting rid of. You can have the nice new ones to-morrow."

If General Trinidad ever guessed how thoroughly improvised his favourite outfit was—the second in command a bank robber on enforced vacation, the gunners kidnapped, the equipment made by forced labour from commandeered material, and the mules snatched rudely from between the shafts of cabs—he made no comment.

He did not live long to enjoy the fruits of my labours. In mid-June, during the ten days' attack which resulted in the fall of Zacatecas, he was mortally wounded.

I shall always remember that day, not only for the death of my chief, but for a personal bit of adventure.

I was temporarily away from my guns with some riflemen in a trench. The enemy fire was very hot and the men became exceedingly restive. Something had to be done to steady them, for there was no cover of any sort on the bullet-

A Hero in Spite of Myself

swept, shrapnel-searched plain behind us. Retreat was impossible. There was plenty of horror in the situation—the blazing sun, the sense of isolation, the cries and curses of the men who were being struck. And there was the cactus.

Unless you have been under fire of high-power rifles in a region where the common broad-leaved cactus grows you cannot guess its nerve-shaking possibilities. A jacketed bullet can pierce a score of leaves without much diminution of its velocity, and as it goes through the thick, juicy flesh, it lets out a sound like the spitting of some gigantic cat. Ten Mauser bullets piercing cactus can make you believe a whole battalion is concentrating its fire on your one small but precious person.

The men were getting demoralised. If they broke I was done for. If I stayed in the trench alone, the Federals would eventually get me and stand me up to the nearest wall. If I retreated, nothing was gained.

I stood up, exposing my body from mid-thigh upwards to that withering fire, and took out my cigarette case. The nearest man watched sidewise, waiting to see me fall.

By some fortune I was not hit, and after a moment looked down at the man beside me.

A Hero in Spite of Myself

"Hallo, Pablo!" I said, "why aren't you smoking too?" I offered my case to him, but took good care to stretch out my arm quite level. To get at the contents he had to rise to his feet.

Habit won. He did not even hesitate, and I held my cigarette, Mexican fashion, for him to take a light. Once committed in that fashion, he was too proud to show the white feather, and he and I smoked our cigarettes out while the bullets flew. It was the longest cigarette, I think, I ever smoked, but it turned the trick. We held on to that trench till darkness put an end to the fire.

After the capture of Zacatecas I went to the staff of General Raul Madero, with the rank of Major. The invitation had been extended several times before. Now that Trinidad was dead, there was nothing to hold me back, and I very gladly joined the official family of the brother of the murdered President. Since my first association with him, before Ojinaga, he had impressed me as the ablest man I had seen south of the Rio Grande.

The closer and more constant contact entailed by my becoming a member of his staff confirmed that feeling. Raul Madero has clarity of intelligence, an encyclopædic grasp of Mexican affairs, social, religious, political and financial, and a

A Hero in Spite of Myself

winning personality that masks abundant energy and determination.

I was associated with him for only six weeks. On June 28, 1914, you remember, the Archduke Francis Ferdinand of Austria was assassinated. Throughout over three weeks of July the Austrian Government was formulating its demands on Serbia which culminated in the ultimatum of July 23. Long before that I had formed my opinion as to which way the wind was to blow. And I had a sufficiently conceited notion of my usefulness as a trained and experienced agent to believe that when the general European disturbance should break out my days as a soldier of fortune in Mexico would be ended.

Towards the end of July a stranger brought me credentials proving him a messenger from Consul Kueck in El Paso.

"The Consul," he told me, "wishes to ask you one question, and the answer is a Yes or a No. This is the question: In case your Government wished your services again, could she expect to receive them?"

"In case of war—Yes," I answered.

It was not very long before I received a telegram from Kueck.

"Come," was all it said.

CHAPTER VII

ENTER CAPTAIN VON PAPEN

War—I re-enter the German service and am appointed aide to Captain von Papen—The German conception of neutrality and how to make use of it—The plot against the Welland Canal.

THE meaning of Kueck's telegram was plain. War had come at last, the war that we had expected and prepared for during so many years. My country was at war and I must leave whatever I was doing and return to its service.

I went to Raul Madero with the telegram.

"It has come," I said. "War! I shall have to go."

We had spoken together too often, during the past few weeks, of my duty in the event of hostilities for any long discussion to be necessary now. I asked for and received all that I believed to be necessary—a leave of absence for six months with the privilege of extension. The next day, August 3, 1914, I said good-bye to my troops and to my commander and hastened north to El Paso.

Enter Captain von Papen

At the Hotel El Paso del Norte I met my former enemies, Kueck and his stout secretary. We had dinner together, and he gave me letters containing instructions to proceed to New York and to place myself at the disposal of Captain Franz von Papen, the German Military Attaché at Washington.

"When will Captain von Papen be in New York?" I asked.

"I have just received a communication from Papen," replied Kueck, adding with a gratified smile, "I am keeping him informed of conditions along the border. He will be in New York two weeks from to-day."

There was no necessity for haste, then, and I remained in El Paso for five days longer, keeping my eyes and ears open and learning, among other things, more "facts" about Mexico than I could have acquired in Mexico itself in a lifetime. "There are lies, damned lies and El Pasograms," someone has said. I collected enough of the last-named to cheer me on my way to Washington and to make me marvel that Rome had ever been called the father of lies. No wonder newspaper correspondents like to report Mexican news from El Paso.

Washington was technically on vacation at the

Enter Captain von Papen

time, but there was an unwonted air of excitement about the city—far greater than formerly existed when Congress was in full session. At the German Embassy I found only a few clerks; but letters from Newport, to which the Ambassador and his staff had gone for the summer, informed me that Captain von Papen would meet me in New York in a fortnight. And then I learned for the first time that it was impossible for me to reach Germany, but that I was to be assigned to work in the United States.

I knew what that meant, of course, and I was not wholly unprepared for it. Secret agents could be very useful in a neutral country, and I knew from my acquaintance with German methods in Europe that plans would already have been made for conserving German interests in the United States. What those plans were I did not know; but my only immediate concern was to remove any possible suspicion from myself by doing something which on the surface would seem to be absolutely idiotic.

I became violently and noisily pro-German. On the train I entered into arguments (as a matter of fact I could not have escaped them if I tried) in which I stoutly defended the invasion of Belgium and prophesied an early victory for

Enter Captain von Papen

Germany. And when I arrived in New York I registered at the Holland House, where my actions would be more conspicuous than at one of the larger hotels, and proceeded to make myself as noticeable as possible by spending a great deal more money than I could afford—and talking.

In a day or two the reporters were on my trail and I became their obliging prey. What I told them I do not now remember in its entirety, but newspaper clippings of the day assure me that I made many wild and bombastic statements, promising that Paris would be captured in a very few weeks—in a word uttering the most flagrant nonsense. The reporters decided that I was a fool and deftly conveyed that impression to their readers. And in a very brief time I had the satisfaction of learning that I was everywhere regarded as a person of considerably more loquacity than intelligence.

That was the very reputation I had attempted to get. I wanted to be known—and widely—as a braggart, a spendthrift, a rattlebrain, for the very excellent reason that in no other way could I so easily divert suspicion from myself later. I was a German, and consequently under the surveillance of enemy secret agents, with whom —oh, believe me!—the United States was filled.

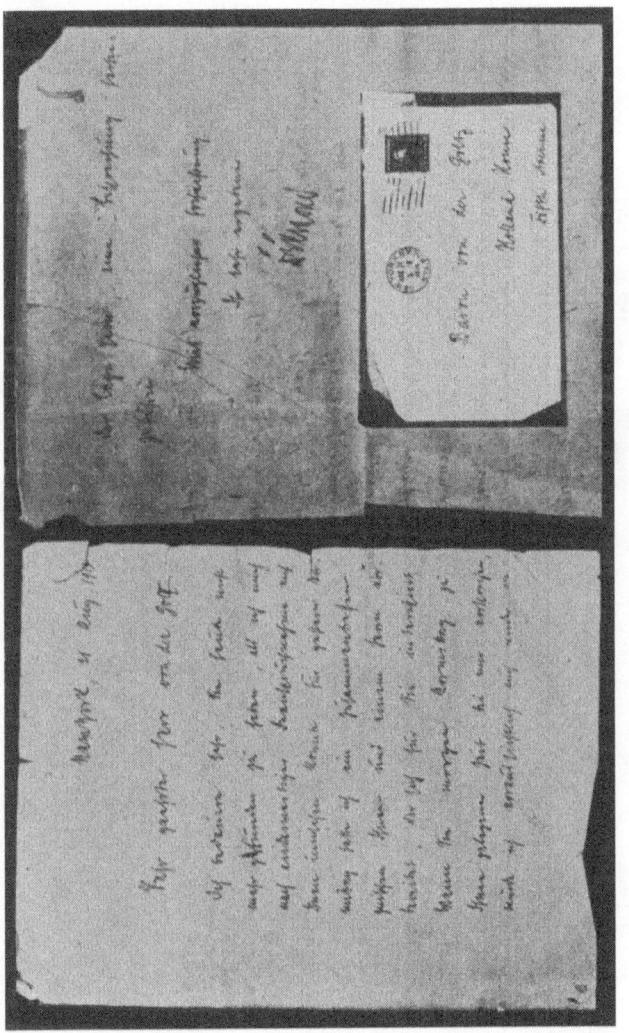

DR. KRASKE'S LETTER TO "BARON" VON DER GOLTZ. (See p. 145)

Enter Captain von Papen

It was impossible for me to escape some notice. Since that was the case, the safest course for me to pursue was to comport myself in such a way that all interested persons would report (as I afterwards learned they did report) that I was not worth watching, since no sane Government would ever employ me.

While I was engaged in achieving this enviable reputation, I had managed to keep in touch with the Imperial German Consulate in New York, and on August 21 I had received from the Vice-Consul, Dr. Kraske, a note informing me that the "gentleman who is interested in you"—Captain von Papen—"will meet you next morning at the Consulate." That letter was to figure two years later in the trial of Captain Hans Tauscher. I reproduce it here. You might note that it is addressed to "Baron von der Goltz," although my card did not bear that title, and I had registered at the Holland House under my Mexican military title of Major.

Upon the following morning I went to that old building at Number Eleven Broadway. There, in a little room in the offices of the Imperial German Consulate, began a series of meetings which were designed to bear fruit of the greatest consequences to the United States—which would,

Enter Captain von Papen

had they been successful, have made American neutrality a lie, and would have perhaps drawn the United States into a serious conflict with England, if not into actual war.

I remember von Papen's enthusiasm as he outlined the general programme to me. "It was merely a question of tying their hands"—that was the burden of his statements, time and again. We could hope for nothing from American neutrality; it was a fraud, a deception. Washington could not see the German view-point at all. Everything was done to favour England. Why, the entire country was supporting the Allies—the Government, the Press, the people—all of them! Nowhere was there a good word for Germany. And that in spite of the excellent propaganda that Germany was conducting. I remember that the failure of German propaganda was an especially sore spot with him.

"How about the German-Americans?" I asked him upon one occasion.

He made a sound that was between a grunt and a cough.

"I am attending to them," was his reply.

I did not understand what he meant until much later.

We talked much of American participation in

Enter Captain von Papen

the war in those days. Papen was convinced that it would come sooner or later; and certainly upon the side of the Entente—unless the German-Americans could be brought into line. They were being attended to, he would repeat, but meanwhile it was necessary for us to decide upon some immediate action. Of course, there was Mexico to be considered. It was too bad that Huerta had fallen. What did I think of Villa? Could he be persuaded to cause a diversion if the United States abandoned its neutrality?

I told him that I thought it very unlikely. "He is not very friendly towards Germans," I said, "and he appreciates the importance of keeping on good terms with the United States. No, I don't think you can reach him—now. Later, he may take a different attitude—when we have had a few more victories."

Von Papen nodded. I was probably right, he thought. We must show these ignorant people how powerful the Germans were. It would have a great moral effect. But that was for the future. In the meantime, what did I think of this letter as a suggestion for possible immediate action?

"This letter" was from a man named Schumacher, who lived in Oregon, at Eden Bower Farm. He had written to the Embassy, suggest-

Enter Captain von Papen

ing that we should secretly fit out motor-boats armed with machine-guns, and using Buffalo, Detroit, Cleveland and Chicago as bases, make raids upon Canadian cities and towns on the Great Lakes.

There were some good features in the plan—its value as a means of terrorising Canadians, for instance—but it was doubtful whether at that time we could carry it out successfully. Then, too, we could not be sure whether it was not merely a trap for us. Papen had been making inquiries about Schumacher and was not entirely satisfied as to his good faith.

There was a number of other schemes which we considered at this time. One was to equip reservists of the German Army, then in the United States, and co-operating with German warships, then in the Pacific Ocean, to invade Canada from the State of Washington. This plan was abandoned because of the impossibility of securing enough artillery for our purposes.

Another plan that we considered more carefully involved an expedition against Jamaica. This was a much more feasible scheme than any that had been proposed thus far, and we spent many days over it. It seemed fairly probable that with an army of ragamuffins which I could easily

Enter Captain von Papen

recruit in Mexico and Central America, we could make a success of it. Arms were easy to secure; in fact, we had a very well equipped arsenal in New York; and filibustering had become so common since the outbreak of the Mexican revolution that it would be easy to obtain what additional material we needed without disclosing our purpose. On the whole, the idea looked promising, and matters had gone so far that von Papen secured my appointment as captain, so that in the event of my being captured on British soil with arms in my hand I should be treated as a prisoner of war.

Then just when we were making final preparations for my departure from New York, von Papen came to me in great excitement and said he had come upon a plan that would serve our purposes to perfection. Canada was, after all, our principal objective; we could strike a telling blow against it, and at the same time create consternation throughout America by blowing up the canals which connected the Great Lakes!

"It is comparatively simple," said von Papen. "If we blow up the locks of these canals the main railway lines of Canada and the principal grain elevators will be crippled. Immediately we shall destroy one of England's chief sources

Enter Captain von Papen

of food supply as well as hamper the transportation of war materials. Canada will be thrown into a panic and public opinion will *demand* that her troops be held for home defence. But, best of all, it will make the Canadians believe that the thousands of German reservists and the millions of German-Americans in the United States are planning active military operations against the Dominion."

I looked at him in surprise. Where had he got such a plan? Papen enlightened me with his next words.

Two men—not Germans but violently anti-English—had come to him with the suggestion, he said. It was in a very indefinite form as yet, but the idea was certainly worth careful consideration. He wished me to discuss the matter with the two men at my hotel.

It did seem a good plan. As I discussed it the next evening with the two men, whom von Papen had sent to me, it seemed entirely practicable and immensely important. Together we went over maps and diagrams, which showed the vulnerable points of the different canals and railways. After a number of conferences with them and with von Papen the plot took definite shape as a plan to blow up the Welland Canal.

Enter Captain von Papen

"It can be done," I told von Papen one day, and together we discussed the details. Finally von Papen looked up from the notes we had been examining.

"I think it will do admirably," he said. "Will you undertake it?"

I nodded.

"Good!" said von Papen. "I shall leave the details to you—but keep me informed of your needs, and I shall see that they are taken care of."

So began the plot which was literally to carry the war into America. My first need was for men, and for help in getting these I appealed to von Papen, who obligingly furnished me with a letter of introduction—made out in the name of Bridgeman H. Taylor—to Mr. Luederitz, the German Consul at Baltimore. There were several German ships interned at that port, and we felt that we should have no difficulty in recruiting our force from them.

Before I went to Baltimore, however, I did engage one man, Charles Tucker, alias Tuchhaendler, who had already had some dealings with the two men who originally proposed the scheme.

Tucker accompanied me to Baltimore, and together we paid a visit to Consul Luederitz. The Consul glanced at the letter I presented to him.

Enter Captain von Papen

"Captain von Papen requests me to give you all the assistance you may ask for, Major von der Goltz," he said, intimating by the use of my name that he had previously been informed of the enterprise. "I shall be happy to do anything in my power. What is it you wish?"

Men, I told him, were my chief need at the moment. He said that there should be no difficulty about securing them. There was a German ship in the harbour at the time, and we could doubtless make use of part of the crew and an officer, if we desired. He offered me his visiting-card, on the back of which he wrote a note of recommendation to the captain of the ship. But while we were talking this man entered the office and we made our preliminary arrangements there.

The following day, a Sunday, Tucker and I visited the ship and after dinner selected our men, who were informed of their prospective duties. I also listened to the news that was being received on board by wireless; for the captain was still allowed to receive messages, although the harbour authorities had forbidden him to use his apparatus for sending purposes.

I needed nothing more in Baltimore, so far as my present plans were concerned, but at Consul Luederitz's suggestion I decided to furnish my-

Enter Captain von Papen

self with a passport, made out in my *nom de guerre* of Bridgeman Taylor. Luederitz was of the opinion that it might be useful at some future time as a means of proving that I was an American citizen, and accordingly we had one of the clerks make out an application, which was duly forwarded to Washington; and on August 31 the State Department furnished the non-existent Mr. Bridgeman H. Taylor with a very comforting, although, as it turned out, a decidedly dangerous document. One other thing I needed at the moment—a pistol, for my own was out of order. This Mr. Luederitz provided me with from the effects of an Austrian who had committed suicide in Baltimore not long before, and whose property, in the absence of an Austrian Consulate in the city, had been turned over to the German Consul.

The days immediately following my return to New York were filled with preparations for our *coup*. I engaged three additional men to act as my lieutenants, acquainted them with the main objects of our plan, and agreed to pay them daily while in New York, and to add a bonus when our enterprise should succeed. These men had all been well recommended to me, and I knew I could trust them thoroughly. One, Fritzen, who was

Enter Captain von Papen

later captured in Los Angeles, had been a purser on a Russian ship. A second, Busse, was a commercial agent who had lived for many years in England; the third bore the Italian name of Covani.

Meanwhile I saw von Papen frequently, and had on one occasion received from him a cheque for two hundred dollars, which I needed for the sailors who were coming from Baltimore. That cheque, which is reproduced in this book, was to prove a singularly disastrous piece of paper, for in order to avoid connecting my name with that of von Papen, it was made out to Bridgeman Taylor. I cashed it through a friend, Frederick Stallforth, whose brother, Alberto Stallforth, had been the German Consul at Parral when I was there. He, incidentally, was later implicated in the Rintelen trial, and was detained for a time on Ellis Island, from which he was subsequently released.

Mr. Stallforth lifted his eyebrows when he saw the name on the cheque. I smiled.

"I am Bridgeman Taylor," I told him. He laughed, but said nothing, merely getting the cheque cashed for me at the German Club in Central Park South, of which he was a member.

In a few days everything was ready. My men had arrived from Baltimore, my plans were

Enter Captain von Papen

definitely made—I needed but one thing: the explosives. These, von Papen told me, I could obtain through Captain Hans Tauscher, the American agent of the Krupps, which meant, in effect, the German Government.

It was asserted many times, in 1916 especially, that the charges against Captain Tauscher were utterly unfounded. It is easy to understand the motives of this gentleman's defenders. There are many people still in the United States whose friendship with the amiable captain would wear a decidedly suspicious look were his complicity in the anti-American plots of the first two years of the war to be proved. I shall not quarrel with these people. But reproduced in this book are four documents, the originals of which are in the possession of the Department of Justice, which tell their own story and are a fair indication of the way I secured the explosives I needed.

These documents show:

First, that on September 5, 1914, Captain Tauscher, American representative of the Krupps, ordered from the du Pont de Nemours Powder Company 300 pounds of 60 per cent dynamite to be delivered to bearer, "Mr. Bridgman Taylor," and to be charged to Captain Tauscher.

Enter Captain von Papen

Second, that on September 11, the du Pont Company sent Captain Tauscher a bill for the same amount of dynamite delivered to Bridgman Taylor, New York City, on September 5; and on September 16 they sent him a second bill for forty-five feet of fuse delivered to Bridgman Taylor on September 13—the total of the two bills amounting to $31.13.

Third, that on December 29, 1914, Tauscher sent a bill to Captain von Papen for a total amount of $503.24. *The third item, dated September 11, was for $31.13.*

Is it difficult to tell of whom I got my explosives or who eventually paid for them? I got the dynamite, at any rate, by calling for it myself at one of the company's barges in a motor boat, and taking it away in suit cases. At 146th Street and the Hudson River we left the boat, and, carrying the explosives with us, went to the German Club, where I applied to von Papen for automatic pistols, batteries, detonators, and wire for exploding the dynamite. Von Papen promised them in two or three days—and he kept his word.*

* It is interesting to remember that Captain von Papen had in the earlier part of the year, while he was still in Mexico, conducted an investigation into the types of explosives used in Mexico for similar enterprises. This investigation had been undertaken at the request

Enter Captain von Papen

Bit by bit, all this material was removed from the German Club—in suit cases by taxi-cab. They were exciting rides we took in those days, and my heart was often in my mouth when our chauffeur turned corners in approved New York fashion. But luckily there were no accidents, and in a day or so all of our materials were stored away; part of them in my apartments—not in the Holland House, alas!—but in a cheap section of Harlem. For von der Goltz, the spendthrift, the braggart, was seen no longer in the gay places of New York. He had spent all his money, and now, no longer of interest to the newspapers—or to the secret agents of the Allies—had taken a two dollar and a half room in Harlem where he could repent his follies—and be as inconspicuous as he pleased.

So it came about that towards the middle of September we five—Fritzen, Busse, Tucker, Covani and myself—took train for Buffalo, armed with dynamite, automatic guns, detonators and other necessary implements, and proceeded, absolutely unmolested, to go to Buffalo. There I engaged rooms at 198 Delaware Avenue and began to reconnoitre the ground. I made

of the German Ministry of War. Letters regarding this matter were found in Captain von Papen's effects by the British authorities, and are printed in the British White Paper, Miscellaneous No. 6 (1916).

Enter Captain von Papen

a trip or two over the Niagara River via aeroplane, with an aviator who unquestionably thought me mad and charged accordingly; and at the suggestion of von Papen I secured money for my expenses from a Buffalo lawyer, John Ryan.

It had been decided that von Papen should let us know when the Canadian troops were about to leave camp so that we might strike at the psychological moment. A telegram came from him, signed with the non-committal name of Steffens, telling me that Ryan had money and instructions. Ryan gave me the money, as I have stated, but insisted that he had no instructions whatever.

Then, after a stay of several days in Niagara, during which we did nothing but exchange futile telegrams with Ryan and "Mr. Steffens," we learned that the first contingent of Canadian troops had left the camp—and my men and I returned to New York unsuccessful.

Our failure was greater than appears on the surface, for my men and I were a blind. Our equipment, our loud talking, our aggressive pro-Germanism—even our secret preparations which had not been secret enough—were intended primarily to distract attention from other and far more dangerous activities.

Enter Captain von Papen

We had been watched by United States Secret Service men from the very beginning of our enterprise. During our entire stay in Buffalo and Niagara we had been under the surveillance of men who were merely waiting for us to make their suspicions a certainty by some positive attempt against the peace of the United States. We *knew* it and wanted it to be so.

And while they were waiting for sufficient cause to arrest us, other men, totally unsuspected, were making their way down through Canada, intent upon destroying *all* of the bridges and canal locks in the lake region!

You can see what the effect would have been had our plan succeeded—Canada crippled and terrorised—England robbed of the troops which Canada was even then preparing to send her, but which would have been forced to remain at home to defend the border. But, far more desirable in German eyes, the United States would have been convicted in the sight of the world of criminal negligence. For my band of men—the obvious perpetrators of one crime—had been acting suspiciously for weeks. And yet, in spite of that, we were at liberty. *The United States had made no effort to apprehend us.*

Good fortune saved the United States from

Enter Captain von Papen

serious international complications at that time. While we were waiting for word from von Papen the Canadian troops had left Valcartier Camp, and were then on their way to England. Part of our object had been removed, and for the rest—well, the plan would keep, we thought.

It was a disappointed von Papen whom I met on my return to New York—a rather crestfallen person, far different from the urbane soldier that Washington knew in those days. We commiserated with each other upon our failure, and talked of the better luck that we should have next time. · I did not know that there was to be no next time for me.

For it came about that Abteilung III. B., the Intelligence Department of the General Staff, wished some first-hand information about conditions in the United States and in Mexico; and I, who knew both countries (and who was the possessor of an American passport bearing an American name), was selected to go.

On October 3, 1914, Bridgeman Taylor waved farewell to New York from the deck of an Italian steamer, bound for Genoa. The curious might have been interested to know that in Mr. Taylor's trunk were letters of recommendation to various German Consuls in Italy;

CAPTAIN VON PAPEN'S LETTER TO THE GERMAN CONSULS AT BALTIMORE AND ST. PAUL

"NEW YORK, 27, viii, 14. I request the Consuls in Baltimore and St. Paul to give the bearer of this letter—Mr. Bridgeman Taylor—all the assistance he may ask for. VON PAPEN, Captain in the General Staff of the Army and Military Attaché."

(*See p.* 151)

Enter Captain von Papen

strangely enough, they bore the name of Horst von der Goltz within them, and the signature of each was "von Papen."

I had said good-bye to von Papen the night before at the German Club. He had asked me to hand over to him all the firearms I had, for use again when needed.

We talked of the war that night, and of Germany, which I had not seen in two years. And we spoke of the United States, and of what I was to tell them "over there."

"Say that they need not worry about this country," he told me. "The United States may still join us in the splendid fight we are making. But if they do not it is of small moment. *And always remember that if things look bad for us, something will happen over here.*"

I left him, speculating upon the "something" that would happen; for then I did not know of all the plans that were in my captain's head. I was to learn more about them later—and I was to know a bitter disgust at the things that men may do in the name of patriotism. But of these matters I will speak in their proper place.

CHAPTER VIII

MY INTERVIEW WITH THE KAISER

I go to Germany on a false passport—Italy in the early days of the war—I meet the Kaiser and talk to him about Mexico and the United States.

IT was peaceful sailing in those early days of the war, and our ship, the *Duca d'Aosta*, reached Genoa without mishap. I had but one moment of trepidation on the voyage, for on the last day the ship was hailed by a British cruiser. Here, I thought, was where I should put my passport to the test but, as it happened, our ship was not searched. An officer came alongside inquiring, among other things, if there were any Germans on board, but he accepted the captain's assurance that there was none—to my intense relief.

Genoa, like all the rest of the world, was in a state of great excitement in those days. Rumours as to the possible course of the Italian Government were flying about everywhere, and one could hear in an hour as many conflicting state-

My Interview with the Kaiser

ments of the Government's intentions as he might wish. The country was a battlefield of the propagandists at the moment. Nearly all of the German Consuls, who had been forced to leave Africa at the declaration of war, had taken up their quarters in Italy, and were busily disseminating pro-German literature of all sorts. I was told, too, that the French Ambassador had already spent large sums of money buying Italian papers in which to present the Allied cause to the as yet neutral people of Italy. And when I went into the office of the Imperial German Consul-General, von Nerf, I was amused to see a huge pile of copies of—of all papers in the world!—the Berlin *Vorwaerts*, which had been imported for distribution throughout the country. Here was a pretty comedy! This newspaper, which during its entire existence had been the bitterest foe of German autocracy in the Empire, had become a propagandist sheet for its former enemy and was now being used as a lure for the hesitating sympathies of the Italian people! In German, French and Italian editions it was spread about the country, carrying the message of Teutonic righteousness to the uninformed.

I found von Nerf to be a large man, with

My Interview with the Kaiser

whiskers that recalled those of Tirpitz, although without that gentleman's temperament or embonpoint. He assured me that Italy would never enter the war; there were too many factions in the country which would oppose such a step.

"Why, consider," he bade me, "we have the three most important parties on our side. The Catholics will never consent to a break with Germany; the business men are all our stanch partisans; and the Labour Party is too violently opposed to war ever to consider entering it. Besides," he continued, "labouring men all over the world know that it is in Germany that the Labour Party has reached its greatest strength. Why, then, should they consider taking sides against us?"

"But do you think that there is any chance of Italy entering the war on our side?" I asked him.

Von Nerf shrugged his shoulders. "It is doubtful," was his reply. "What could they do in their situation?"

I had come to von Nerf with von Papen's letter of introduction, to ask for assistance in reaching Germany. Accordingly he arranged for my passage, and soon I was on a train bound for Milan and Kufstein, where I was to change for the train to Munich. At that time the German

My Interview with the Kaiser

Consuls were paying the passage of thousands of Germans who wished to leave Italy for service in the army. The train on which I travelled was full of these volunteers, who later disembarked at Kufstein, on the Austro-German border, to report to the military authorities there.

At Munich we passed some wounded who were being taken from the front—the first real glimpse of the war that I had had. There was little evidence of any war feeling in the Bavarian capital; restaurants were crowded, and everyone was light-hearted and confident of victory. I saw few signs of any hatred there, or elsewhere during my stay in Germany. All that there was was directed against England; France was universally respected, and I heard only expressions of regret that she was in the war.

On the train from Munich to Berlin I had the first good meal I had eaten in several weeks. It was good to sit down to something besides miles of spaghetti and indigestible anchovies. And the price was only two marks—for that was long before the days of the Food Controller and $45 ham.

Berlin was filled with Austrian officers, some of them belonging to motor batteries—the famous '32's—which had been built before the war in the

My Interview with the Kaiser

Krupp factories, not for Germany—for that would have occasioned additional armaments on the part of France—but by Austria, who could increase her strength without suspicion. The city, always martial in appearance, had changed less than one would have expected. There, too, the restaurants were filled; in particular the Piccadilly, which had been rechristened the Fatherland, and was enjoying an exceptional popularity in consequence. One was wise to go early if he wished to secure a table there; and that fortunate person could see the dining-room filled with happy crowds, eating and drinking, and applauding vociferously when "Die Wacht am Rhein" or some other patriotic air was played.

I had returned to Germany for two purposes: to fight, and to bring full details of conditions in Mexico and the United States to the War Office. One of my first official visits was paid to the Foreign Office, where I found everyone busy with routine matters and very little concerned about the success or failure of the German propaganda in Italy—an attitude in marked contrast to that of the General Staff. There the first question asked of me related to conditions in Italy. This indifference of the Foreign Office would seem, in the light of after events, to in-

My Interview with the Kaiser

dicate a false security on the Ministry's part; but in reality the facts are otherwise. Germany had never expected Italy to enter the war on the side of the Central Powers; she did hope that her former ally would remain neutral, and at that time was doing her utmost to keep her so, both by propaganda and by assuring her of a supply of coal and other commodities, for which Italy had formerly depended upon England, and which Germany now hoped to secure for her from America. But even at the time of my visit the indications of Italy's future course were fairly clear—and the Foreign Office was accepting its failure with as good grace as it could.

But if the Foreign Office were indifferent to the attitude of Italy, it was intensely interested in that of Turkey, which had not yet entered the war. It seemed to me as if Mannesmann and Company, a house whose interests in the Orient are probably more extensive than those of any other German company, seemed almost to have taken possession of the Colonial Office, so many of its employees were in evidence there; and I had an extended conference with Bergswerkdirektor Steinmann, who had formerly been in charge of the Asia Minor interests of this company. Mexico, of course, was the principal topic of our

My Interview with the Kaiser

conversation, but many times he spoke of Turkey and of the small doubt that existed as to her future course of action.

Next door to the Foreign Office, every corner of which was a-hum with busy clerks and officials, stood the house to which I had been taken from Gross Lichterfelde so many years before—"Samuel Meyer's Bude." It was very quiet and empty to outward appearance; and yet from within that silent, deserted house, I think it safe to say, the destiny of Europe was being directed. It was there that the Kaiser spent his days when he was in Berlin. And it was there that the Imperial Chancellor had his office and determined more than any man, except the Kaiser, the policies of the Empire.

One entered the house, going directly into a large room that was occupied no longer by the round-faced man of my cadet days, but by Assessor Horstman, the head of the Intelligence Department of the Foreign Office. Upstairs was the private office of the Emperor, and, to the rear of that, the Nachrichten Bureau—a newspaper propaganda and intelligence office, directed by the Kaiser and under the charge of Legation-Secretary Weber.

I visited the Turkish Legation, at the sugges-

My Interview with the Kaiser

tion of Herr Steinmann, and discussed at length and very seriously with the Ambassador the attitude of Italy and its effect upon Turkey's possible entry into the war. He assured me that the only thing necessary to make Turkey take part in the conflict was a guarantee that Germany was capable of handling the Italian situation, and that whatever Italy might do would not affect Turkish interests.

But it was with the General Staff that my chief business was. At the outbreak of hostilities this —the "War Office" so-called—had become two organisations. One, devoted to the actual supervision of the forces in the field, had its headquarters in Charleville, France, far behind the battle front; the other branch remained in the dingy old building on the Koenig's Platz, in which it had always been quartered. It is here that the army department of "Intelligence," officially known as Abteilung III. B, is located, and it was to this department that I had been assigned.

Von Papen had, of course, communicated to Berlin an account of our various activities, and there was little that I could add to the information the department possessed about conditions in the United States. Mexico seemed rather the

My Interview with the Kaiser

chief point of interest, and Major Köhnemann, to whom I spoke, asked innumerable questions about the attitude of Villa towards both the United States and Germany; what I thought of his chances of ultimate success, and whether I believed that he, if he succeeded, would be more friendly to Germany than Carranza was at the time. After an hour of such discussion, which more closely resembled a cross-examination, he suddenly rose.

"Your information is of great interest, Captain von der Goltz," he said. "I shall ask you to return here at five o'clock this evening. Wear your heaviest underclothing. You are going to see the Emperor."

I started. Prussian officers do not joke as a rule, but for the life of me I could not see any sane connection between his last two remarks. The major must have noticed my perplexity, for he smiled as he continued:

"You are going to travel by Zeppelin," he explained. "It will be very cold."

That night I drove by motor to a point on the outskirts of the city, where a Zeppelin was moored. It was one of those which had formerly been fitted up for passenger service, and was now used when quick transportation of a small number of men

My Interview with the Kaiser

was necessary. There were several officers of the General Staff whose immediate presence at Coblenz, where the Emperor had stationed himself, was needed; and since speed was essential we were to travel in this way.

The miles lying between Berlin and Coblenz seemed but so many rods to me, as I sat in the saloon of the great airship, resting and talking to my fellow-passengers. One would have thought that we had been travelling but a few moments when suddenly there loomed below us in the moonlight the twin fortresses of Ehrenbreitstein and Coblenz, each built upon a high plateau. Between them, in the valley, the lights of the city shone dimly; in the centre of the town was the Schloss, where the Emperor awaited us.

But I did not see the Emperor that night. Instead, I was shown to a room in the castle—a room lighted by candle—and there my attendant bade me good night.

At half-past three I was awakened by a knock at the door. " Please dress," said a voice. " His Majesty wishes to see you at four o'clock."

It was still dark when at four o'clock I entered that room on the ground floor of the castle where the Emperor of Emperors worked and ate and slept. In the dim light I saw him, bent over a

My Interview with the Kaiser

table on which was piled correspondence of all kinds. He did not seem to have heard me enter the room, and as he continued to work, signing paper after paper with great rapidity, I looked down and noticed that, in my haste to appear before him on time, I had dressed completely save for one thing. I was in my stocking feet.

I coughed to announce my presence. He looked up then, and I saw that he wore a Litewka, that undress military jacket which is used by soldiers for stable duty, and which German officers wear sometimes in their homes. But the face that met mine startled me almost out of my composure; for it was more like the countenance of Pancho Villa than that of Wilhelm Hohenzollern. That face, as a rule so majestic in its expression, was drawn and lined; his hair was disarranged and showed numerous bald patches which it ordinarily covered. And his moustache—for so many years the target of friend and foe—which was always pointed so arrogantly upwards, drooped down and gave him a dispirited look which I had never seen him wear before.

In a word, it was an extremely nervous and not a stolid Teutonic person who sat before me in that room. And it was not an assertive, but

My Interview with the Kaiser

merely a very tired human being who finally addressed me.

"I am sorry to have been obliged to call you at this hour," he said, "but I am very busy, and it is important that I should see you."

And then, instead of ordering me to report to him, instead of commanding me to tell him those things which I had been sent to tell him, this autocrat, this so-called man of iron, spoke to me as one man to another, almost as a friend speaks to a friend.

I do not remember all that we spoke of in that half-hour—the three years that have passed have brought me too much of experience for me to recall clearly more than the general tenor of our conversation. It is his manner that I remember most vividly, and the general impression of the scene. For as I stood before him then, it suddenly seemed to me that he spoke and looked as a man will who is confronted by a problem that for the moment has staggered him—not because of its immensity, but because he sees now that he has always misunderstood it.

Here, I thought, is a man accustomed to facing all issues with grand words and a show of arrogance; and now at a time when oratory is of no avail, he finds himself still indomitable, per-

My Interview with the Kaiser

haps, but a trifle lost, a trifle baffled, when he contemplates the work before him. For Wilhelm II. had laboured for years to prevent, or if that were impossible, to come victoriously through, the crisis which he knew must some day develop, and which he himself had at last precipitated. He had striven constantly to entrench Germany in a position that would command the world; and had sought to concentrate, so far as may be, the trouble spots of the world into one or two, to the end that Germany, when the time came, might extinguish them at a blow. But the time had come, and he knew that, despite his efforts, there were not two, but many issues that must be faced, and each one separately. He had striven with a sort of perverted altruism to prepare the world for those things which he believed to be right and which, therefore, must prevail. And now after long years of preparation, of diplomatic intrigue with its record of nations bribed, threatened, or cajoled into submission or alliance, he was faced with a condition which gave the lie to his expectations, and he knew that "failure" must be written across the years. Russia and Japan were for the moment lost; Italy was making ready to cut itself loose from that alliance which had been so insecurely founded upon mistrust. And in

My Interview with the Kaiser

America—who could tell? And yet for all that I read weariness and bewilderment in his every tone, I could find in him no trace of hesitation or uncertainty. Instead, I knew that running through every fibre of the man there was an unquestioning assurance of victory—a victory that must come!

While I stood there imagining these things, he spoke of our aims in Europe and in America and of the things that must be done to bring them to success. He bade me tell him the various details of our affairs in Mexico and the United States; and he, like Köhnemann, was chiefly interested in Mexico. It was, in fact, almost suspicious, his interest was so great; and I could explain it only in one way—that he viewed Mexico as the ultimate battlefield of Japan and the United States in the next great struggle—the struggle for the mastery of the Pacific. For just as Belgium has been the battlefield of Europe, so must Mexico be the battleground of America in that war which the future seems to be preparing.

I remember wondering, as he spoke of what might come to pass, at the tremendous familiarity he displayed with the points of view of the peoples and Governments of both Americas. I had thought myself well acquainted with condi-

My Interview with the Kaiser

tions in both continents; but here was a man separated by thousands of miles from the peoples of whom he talked, whose knowledge was, nevertheless, more correct, as I saw it, than that of anyone—Dernburg not excepted—whom I had met.

It was then, I think, that he told me what Germany wished of me, outlining briefly those things which he thought I could do best.

"You can serve us," he said, "in Turkey or in America. In the one you will have an opportunity to fight as thousands of your countrymen are fighting. In the other, you will have chosen a task that is not so pleasant, perhaps, and not less dangerous, but which will always be regarded honourably by your Emperor, because it is work that must be done. Which do you choose?"

I hesitated a moment.

"It shall be as your Majesty wishes," I said finally.

He looked at me closely before he spoke again. "It is America, then."

And then, as I bowed in acquiescence, he spoke once more—for the last time so far as my ears are concerned.

"I must be ready by 7; my train leaves at 7.10. I may never see you again, but I shall

BILLS FROM THE DU PONT DE NEMOURS POWDER COMPANY FOR
"MERCHANDISE" DELIVERED TO "BRIDGEMAN TAYLOR" AND
CHARGED TO CAPTAIN TAUSCHER. (*See pp.* 155-6)

My Interview with the Kaiser

always know that you have done your duty. Good-bye!"

And so I left him—this man who is a menace to his people, not because he is vicious or from any criminal intent; not, I believe, because his personal ambitions are such that his country must bleed to satisfy them; but merely because his mind is the outcome of a system and an education so divorced from fact that he could not see the evil of his own position if it were explained to him.

For in spite of his remarkable grasp of the facts of Empire, the deeper human realities have passed him by. For years he has had a private clipping bureau for his own information; but he does not know that he has never seen any but the clippings that the Junkers—those who stood to gain by the success of his present course—have wished him to see. He does not know that he has been shut out from many chapters of the world's real history; or that this insidious censorship has kept from him those things which, I am sure, had he known in the days when his intellect was susceptible to the influence of fact, would have made him a man instead of an Emperor.

Here was a man who honestly believed that he was doing what was best for his people, but so

My Interview with the Kaiser

hopelessly warped by his training and so closely surrounded by satellites that even had the truth borne wings it could not have reached him.

To me it seems that the menace of the Hohenzollerns lies in this: not that they are worse than other men, not that they mean ill to the world, but that time and experience have left them unaroused by what others know as progress. They stand in the pathway of the world to-day, believing themselves right and regarding themselves as victims of an oppressive rivalry. They do not know that their viewpoint is as tragically perverted as that of the fox which, feeling that it must live, steals the farmer's hens. But, like the farmer, the world knows only that it is injured; and just as the farmer realises that he must rid himself of the fox, so the world knows, to-day, and says that the Hohenzollerns must go!

CHAPTER IX

MY ARREST AND CONFESSION

In England, and how I reached there—I am arrested and imprisoned for fifteen months—What von Papen's baggage contained.—I make a sworn statement.

BACK in Berlin I sought out Major Köhnemann, and together we spent many days in planning my future course of action. It was a war council in effect, for the object towards which we aimed was nothing less than the crippling of the United States by a campaign of terrorism and conspiracy. It was not pleasant work that I was to do, but I knew, as every informed German did, that it was necessary. Therefore I accepted it.

What would you have? Germany was in the war to conquer or be conquered. America, the source of supply for the Allies, stood in the way. Knowing these things, we set about the task of preventing America from aiding our enemies by using whatever means we could. We did not feel either compunction or hostility. It was war —diplomatic rather than military, but war none the less.

My Arrest and Confession

I do not intend to go into the details of our plans at the present moment. Enough to say that after a brief visit to both the Eastern and Western fronts I left Germany for England—*en route* to America with a programme which, in ruthlessness or efficiency, left nothing to be desired.

But before going to England it was necessary that I should take every possible precaution against exposure there. My passport might be sufficient identification, but I knew that since the arrest of Carl Lody and other German spies in England the British authorities were examining passports with a great deal more care than they had formerly exercised. Accordingly, one morning, Mr. Bridgeman Taylor presented himself at the American Embassy for financial aid with which to leave Germany. There was good reason for this. To ask a Consulate or Embassy to visé a passport when that is not necessary may easily seem suspicious. But the applicant for aid receives not only additional identification in the form of a record of his movements, but also secures an advantage in that his passport bears an endorsement of his appeal for assistance, in my case signed with the name of the Ambassador. At The Hague I again applied for help from the United States Relief Commission. I amused

My Arrest and Confession

myself on this occasion by making two drafts: one for $15 on Mr. John F. Ryan of Buffalo, N.Y., and one for $80 on "Mr. Papen" of New York City.

I was fairly secure, then, I thought. If suspicion did fall upon me it would be simple to prove that I had submitted my passport to a number of American officials, and had consequently satisfied them of my good faith as well as that the passport had not been issued to someone other than myself, as in the case of Lody.

As a final step I took care to divide my personal papers into two groups: those which were perfectly harmless, such as my Mexican commission and leave of absence, and those which would tend to establish my identity as a German agent. These I deposited in two separate safe deposit vaults in Rotterdam, taking care to remember in which each group was placed—and that done, with a feeling of personal security, and even a certain amount of zest for the adventure, I boarded a Channel steamer for England.

I was absolutely safe, I felt. In my confidence I went about very freely, ignoring the fact that England was at the moment in the throes of a spy scare, and even so well recom-

My Arrest and Confession

mended a German-American as Mr. Bridgeman Taylor was not likely to escape scrutiny.

And yet, I believe that I should not have been caught at all if I had not stopped one day in front of the Horse Guards and joined the crowd that was watching guard mount. Why I did it it is impossible for me to say. There was no military advantage to be gained; that is certain. And I had seen guard mount often enough to find no element of novelty in it. Whim, I suppose, drew me there; and as luck would have it, it drew me into a particularly congested portion of the crowd. And then chance played another card by causing a small boy to step on my foot. I lost my temper and abused the lad roundly for his carelessness—so roundly, in fact, that a man standing in front of me turned and looked into my face.

I recognised him at once as an agent of the Russian Government, whom I had once been instrumental in exposing as a spy in Germany. I saw him look at me closely for a moment, and I could tell by his expression, although he said no word, that he had recognised me also. Thrusting a penny into the boy's hand I made haste to get out of the crowd as quickly as I could.

My Arrest and Confession

Here was a pleasant situation, I thought, as I made my way very quietly to my hotel. I could not doubt that the Russian would report me—but what then? His word against mine would not convict me of anything, but it might lead to an inconvenient period of detention. I sat down to consider the situation.

After all, I decided, the situation was serious but not absolutely hopeless. Unquestionably I should be reported to the police; unquestionably a careful investigation would result in the discovery that there was no Bridgeman H. Taylor at the address in El Paso which I had given to the Relief Commission at The Hague. For the rest, my accent would prove only that I was of German blood; not that I was a German subject.

So far, so bad. But what then? I had, in the safe deposit vaults in Rotterdam, papers proving that I was a Mexican officer on leave. It would be a simple matter to send for these papers, to admit that I was Horst von der Goltz, and to state that I was in England *en route* from a visit to my family in Germany and now bound for Mexico to resume my services. There remained but one matter to explain: why I was using an American passport bearing a name that was not mine.

My Arrest and Confession

That should not be a difficult task. Huerta had been overthrown barely a week before my leave of absence was issued. Carranza's Government had not yet been recognised, and already my general, Villa, had quarrelled with him, so that it was impossible for me to procure a passport from the Mexican Government. In my dilemma I had taken advantage of the offer of an American exporter, who had been kind enough to lend me his passport, which he had secured and found he did not need at the time. As for my name, it was not a particularly good one under which to travel in England, so I had naturally been obliged to use the one on my passport.

It was a good story and had somewhat the appearance of truth. The question was, would it be believed? Even if it were, it had its disadvantages; for I should certainly be arrested as an enemy alien, and after a delay fatal to all my plans, I should probably be deported. I decided to try a bolder scheme.

In Parliamentary White Paper, Miscellaneous No. 13 (1916), you will find a statement which explains my next step.

"Horst von der Goltz," it says, "arrived in England from Holland on November 4, 1914. He offered information upon projected air raids,

My Arrest and Confession

the source whence the *Emden* derived her information as to British shipping, and how the *Leipzig* was obtaining her coal supply. *He offered to go back to Germany to obtain information, and all he asked for in the first instance was his travelling expenses.*"

What is the meaning of these amazing statements? Simply this. I realised that even if the story I had concocted were believed it would mean a considerable delay and ultimate deportation. And as I had no mind to submit to either of these things if I could avoid them, I decided to forestall my Russian friend by taking the only possible step—one commendable for its audacity if for nothing else. Accordingly I walked straight to Downing Street and into the Foreign Office. I asked to see Mr. X, of the Secret Intelligence Department. This was walking into the jaws of the lion with a vengeance.

I told Mr. X that I wished to enter the British Secret Service; that I was in a position to secure much valuable information.

" Upon what subject? "

Zeppelin raids, I told him. I chose that subject first, because it was the least harmful I could think of in case my "traitorous" offer ever reached the ear of Berlin. No one knew better

My Arrest and Confession

than I how impossible it was to obtain information about Zeppelins. I reasoned that the officers in command of Abteilung III. B in the General Staff would know that I was bluffing when I offered to get information upon that subject for the English. They would know that I was not in a position to have or to obtain any such knowledge, for in Germany no topic is so closely guarded as that. Also, I reasoned that it was a topic in which the English were vastly interested. They were.

Mr. X was hesitating, so I added two other equally absurd subjects: the movements of the *Emden* and the *Leipzig*, about which I knew—and the service chiefs knew that I knew—absolutely nothing.

Mr. X was plainly puzzled. My intentions seemed to be good. At any rate, I had come to him quite openly, and any ulterior motives I might have had were not apparent. Then, too, I had offered him the key of my safe deposit box, telling him what it contained. He considered a moment.

"We shall have to investigate your story," he said finally. "We shall send to Holland for the papers you say are contained in the vault there; and you will be questioned further. In

My Arrest and Confession

the meantime I shall have to place you under arrest."

I had expected nothing better than this, and went to my gaol with a feeling that was relief rather than anything else. My papers would establish my identity, and then, if all went well, I should go back to Germany and make my way to America by another route.

But all did not go well. Somehow, in spite of my commission and leave of absence—perhaps because my offer seemed too good to be true— the British authorities decided that it would be better to lose the information I had offered them and keep me in England. Whatever their suspicions, the only charge they could bring against me and prove was that I was an alien enemy who had failed to register. They had no proof whatever of any connection between me and the German Government. So on November 13, 1914, they brought me into a London police-court to answer the charge of failing to register. I was delighted to do so. It was far more comfortable than facing a court-martial on trial for my life as a spy, as the English newspapers had seemed to expect. Accordingly on November 26 I was duly sentenced to six months' hard labour in Pentonville Prison, with a recommendation for

My Arrest and Confession

deportation at the expiration of my sentence. I served five months at Pentonville, and then my good behaviour let me out.

Home Secretary McKenna signed the order for my deportation. I was free. I was to slip from under the paw of the lion.

And then something happened—to this day I don't know what. Instead of being deported I was thrust into Brixton Prison, where Kuepferer hanged himself, strangely enough, just after his troubles seemed over. Kuepferer had driven a bargain with the English. He was to give them information in return for his life and freedom; and then, when he had everything arranged, he committed suicide. In Brixton I was not sentenced on any charge, I was simply held in solitary confinement, with occasional diversions in the form of a "third degree." After my first insincere offer to give the English information I kept my mouth shut and made no overtures to them, although I confess that the temptation to tell all I knew was often very great. The English got nothing out of me, and in September, 1915, I was shifted to another prison. They took me out of Brixton and placed me in Reading gaol—the locale of Oscar Wilde's ballad. Conditions were less disagreeable there. I was allowed to

My Arrest and Confession

have newspapers and magazines, and to talk and exercise with my fellow-prisoners.

You may be sure that all this time the English made attempts to solve my personal identity as well as to learn the reason for my being in England. They could not shake my story. Time after time I told them: "I am Horst von der Goltz, an officer of the Mexican army on leave. I used the United States passport made out to Bridgeman Taylor from necessity—to avoid the suspicion that would be attached to me because of my German descent.

"Gentlemen, that is all I can tell you."

Over and over again I repeated that meagre statement to the men who questioned me. I would not tell them the truth, and I knew that no lie would help me. And then came an event which changed my viewpoint and made me tell—if not the whole story—at least a considerable part of it.

I had, as I have said, managed to secure newspapers in my new quarters. It is difficult to say how eagerly I read them after so many months of complete ignorance, or with what anxiety I studied such war news as came into my hands. It was America in which I was chiefly interested, for I knew that after my capture some other

My Arrest and Confession

man must have been sent to do the work which I had planned to do. I know now that it was von Rintelen who was selected—that infinitely resourceful intriguer who planted his spies throughout the United States, and for a time seemed well on the way to succeeding in the most gigantic conspiracy against a peaceful nation that had ever been undertaken. But at the time I could tell nothing of this, although I watched unceasingly for reports of strikes, explosions and German uprisings which would tell me that that work which I had been commanded to do, and from which I was only too glad to be spared, was being prosecuted.

So several months passed—months in which I had time for meditation and in which I began to see more clearly some things which had been hinted at in Berlin—and of which I shall tell more later. And then one day I read a dispatch that caused me to sit very silently for a moment in my cell, and to wonder—and fear a little.

Von Papen had been recalled.

I read the story of how he and Captain Boy-Ed had overreached and finally betrayed themselves; of the passport frauds they had conducted; of the conspiracies and seditions they had sought to stir up. I learned that they had been sent home

My Arrest and Confession

under a safe-conduct which did not cover any documents they might carry. It was this last fact which caused me uneasiness. Had von Papen, always so confident of his success, attempted to smuggle through some report of his two years of plotting? It seemed improbable, and yet, knowing his tendency to take chances, I was troubled by the possibility. For such a report might contain a record of my connection with him—and I was not protected by a safe-conduct!

My fears were well founded, as you know. Von Papen carried with him no particular reports, but a number of personal papers which were seized when his ship stopped at Falmouth.

In my prison I read of the seizure and was doubly alarmed; increasingly so when the newspapers began publishing reports which implicated literally hundreds of Irish- and German-Americans whose services von Papen had used in his plots. Then as the days passed, and my name was not mentioned in the disclosures, I became relieved.

"After all," I thought, "he knows that I am here in prison and that I have kept silent. He will have been careful. These others—he has had some reason for his incautiousness with them.

My Arrest and Confession

But he will not betray me, just as he has betrayed none of his German associates."

Then, on the night of January 30, 1916, the governor of Reading prison informed me that I was to go to London the next day.

"Where to?" I asked.

"To Scotland Yard," he said briefly.

"What for?"

"I do not know."

My heart sank, for I realised at once that something had occurred which was of vital import to me. I have faced firing squads in Mexico. I have stood against a wall waiting for the signal that should bid the soldiers fire. And I have taken other dangerous chances without, I believe, more fear than another man would have known. But never have I felt more reluctant than that night when I stood outside of Scotland Yard, waiting—for what?

I was brought into the office of the Assistant Commissioner and found myself in the presence of four men, who regarded me gravely and in silence.

There was something tomb-like about the atmosphere of the room, I thought, as I faced these men—and then I changed my opinion, for I saw lying open on the table around which they were

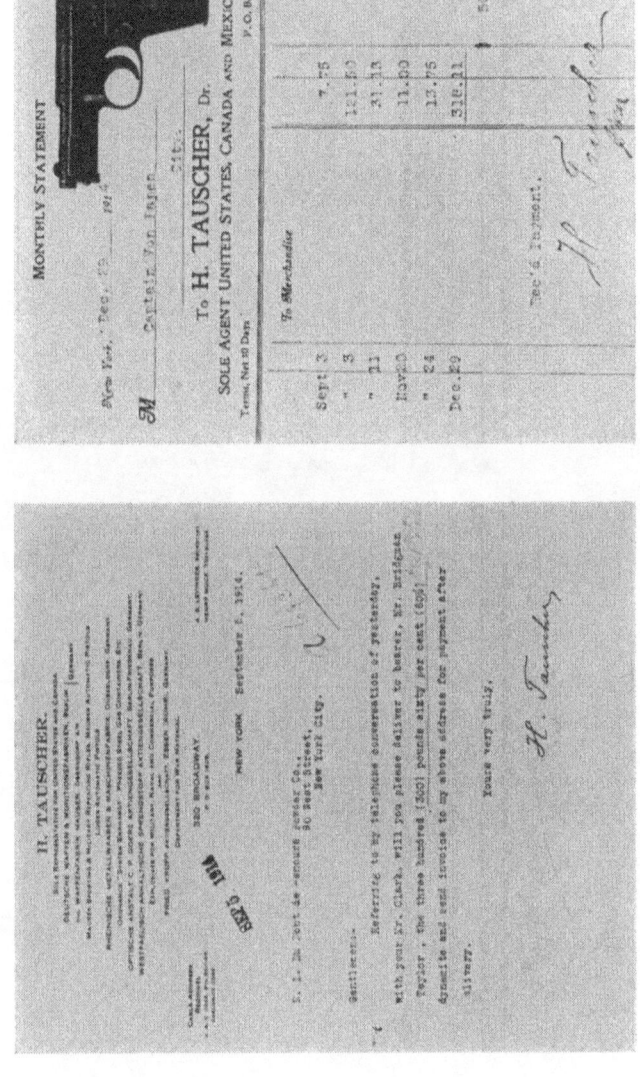

CAPTAIN TAUSCHER'S ORDER FOR "EXPLOSIVES" (Left) AND OF HIS ACCOUNT (Right) TO CAPTAIN VON PAPEN FOR "MERCHANDISE." (See pp. 155-6)

My Arrest and Confession

seated a box of cigarettes. I reached forward to take one, forgetting all politeness (for I had not smoked for six weeks), when my eye caught sight of a little pink slip of paper which one of them held in his hand—a slip which, I knew at once, was the cause of my presence there.

It read:

"WASHINGTON, D.C.
"September 1, 1914.
"The Riggs National Bank,
"Pay to the order of Mr. Bridgeman Taylor two hundred dollars.
"F. VON PAPEN."

One of the company turned over the cheque so that I could see the endorsement.

They were all watching me. The room was very still. I could hear myself breathe. They handed me a pen and paper.

"Sign this name, please—Mr. Bridgeman Taylor."

I knew it would be folly to attempt to disguise my handwriting. I wrote out my name. It corresponded exactly with the endorsement on the back of the cheque.

"Do you know that cheque?" I was asked.

"Yes," I admitted, racking my wits for a possible explanation of the affair.

My Arrest and Confession

" Why was it issued? "

I had an inspiration.

" Von Papen gave it to me to go to Europe and join the army—but you see I didn't——"

" Ah! Von Papen gave it to you."

I was doing quick thinking. My first fright was over, but I realised that that little cheque might easily be my death-warrant. I knew that von Papen had many reports and instructions bearing my name. I was afraid to admit to myself that after all these months of security I had at last been discovered. Von Papen's cheque proved that I had received money from a representative of the German Government. There might be other papers which would prove everything needed to sentence me to execution. I was groping around for an idea—and then in a flash I realised the truth. It angered and embittered me.

There passed across my memory the year and more of solitary confinement, during which I had held my tongue.

I swung around on the Englishmen.

" Are you the executioners of the German Government? " I asked. " Are you so fond of von Papen that you want to do him a favour? If you shoot me you will be obliging him."

My Arrest and Confession

"We are going to prosecute you on this evidence," was the only answer.

"You English pride yourselves," I said, "on not being taken in. Von Papen is a very clever man. Are you going to let him use you for his own purposes? Do you think he was foolish enough not to realise that those papers would be seized? Do you think"—this part of it was a random shot, and lucky—"do you think it is an accident that the only papers he carried referring to a live, unsentenced man in England refer to me? Just think! Von Papen has been recalled. The United States can investigate his actions now without embarrassment. And he, knowing me to be one of the connecting links in the chain of his activities, and knowing that I am a prisoner liable to extradition, would ask nothing better than to be permanently rid of me. And in the papers he carried he very obligingly furnished you with incriminating evidence against me. You can choose for yourselves. Do him this favour if you want to. But I think I'm worth more to you alive than dead. Especially now that I see how very willing my own Government is to have me dead."

My hearers exchanged glances. I had made the appeal as a forlorn hope. Would they accept

My Arrest and Confession

it and the promise it implied? I could not tell from their next words.

"We shall discuss that further. Meanwhile, you will return to Reading."

The next few days were full of anxiety. I could not tell how my appeal had been regarded, but I knew that it would be only by good fortune that I should escape at least a trial for espionage—for that is what my presence in England would mean. Finally, I received a tentative assurance of immunity if I should tell what I knew of the workings of German secret agencies.

In spite of any hesitancy I might formerly have felt at such a course, I decided to make a confession. Von Papen's betrayal of me—for that he had intentionally betrayed me I was, and am, convinced—was too wanton to arouse in me any feeling except a desire for my freedom, which for fifteen months I had been robbed of merely through the silence which my own sense of honour imposed upon me. But I must be careful. I had no desire to injure anyone whom von Papen had not implicated. And I did not wish to betray any secret which I could safely withhold.

I speculated upon what other documents von Papen might have carried. So far as I knew the only one involving me was the cheque; but of that

My Arrest and Confession

I could not be sure, nor did it seem likely. It was more probable that there were other papers which would be used to test the sincerity of my story. My aim was to tell only such things as were already known, or were quite harmless. But how to do that? I needed some inkling as to what I might tell and on what I must be silent.

That knowledge was difficult to obtain, but I finally secured it through a rather adroit questioning of one of the men who interrogated me at the time. He had shown me much courtesy and no little sympathy; and after some pains I managed to worm out of him a very indefinite but useful idea of what matters the von Papen documents covered.

What I learned was sufficient to enable me to exclude from my story any facts implicating men who might be harmed by my disclosures. I told of the Welland Canal plot so far as my part in it was concerned, and I told of von Papen's share in that and other activities. And I took care to incorporate in my confession the promise of immunity that had been made me tentatively.

"I have made these statements," I wrote, "on the distinct understanding that the statements I have made, or should make in the future, will not be used against me; that I am not to be prosecuted

My Arrest and Confession

for participation in any enterprise directed against the United Kingdom or her Allies which I engaged in at the direction of Captain von Papen or other representatives of the German Government; and that the promise that I am not to be extradited or sent to any country where I am liable to punishment for political offences, is made on behalf of His Majesty's Government."

It was on February 2 that I completed my confession and swore to the truth of it. Affairs went better with me after that. I was sent to Lewes prison, and there I was content for the remainder of my stay in England. And although I was still a prisoner I felt more free than I had felt for many years. I was out of it all—free of the necessity to be always watchful, always secret. And, above all, I had cut myself adrift from the intriguing which once I had enjoyed, but which in the last two years I had grown to hate more than I hated anything else on earth.

And there my own adventures end—so far as this book is concerned. I shall not do more than touch upon my return to the United States on a far different errand from that I had once planned. My testimony in the Grand Jury proceedings against Captain Tauscher, von Igel, and others of my onetime fellow-conspirators, is a matter of

My Arrest and Confession

too recent record to deserve more than passing mention. Tauscher, you will remember, was acquitted because it was impossible to prove that he was aware of the objects for which he had supplied explosives. Von Igel, Captain von Papen's secretary, was protected by diplomatic immunity. And Fritzen and Covani, my former lieutenants, had not yet been captured.*

But though my intriguing was ended, Germany's was not. It may be interesting to consider these intrigues, in the light of what I had learned during those two years—and what I have discovered since.

* Fritzen, who was captured in Hartwood, Cal., on March 9, 1917, was arraigned in New York City on March 16, and after pleading not guilty, later reversed his plea. He was sentenced to a term of eighteen months in a Federal prison.

CHAPTER X

GERMANY'S HATE CAMPAIGN IN AMERICA

The German intrigue against the United States—Von Papen, Boy-Ed, and von Rintelen, and the work they did—How the German-Americans were used, and how they were betrayed.

IN the long record of German intrigue in the United States one fact stands out predominantly. If you consider the tremendous ramifications of the system which Germany has built, the extent of its organisation and the efficiency with which so gigantic a secret work was carried on, you will realise that this system was not the work of a short period, but of many years. As a matter of fact, Germany had laid the foundation of that structure of espionage and conspiracy many years before—even before the time when the United States first became a Colonial Power and thus involved herself in the tangle of world politics.

I am making no rash assertions when I state that ten years ago the course which German agents should adopt towards the United States in the event of a great European war had been deter-

Germany's Hate Campaign

mined with a reasonable amount of exactness by the General Staff, and that it was this plan which was adapted to the conditions of the moment, and set into operation at the outbreak of the present conflict. No element of hostility lay behind this planning. Germany had no grievance against America; and whatever potential causes of conflict existed between the two nations lay in the far future.

That plan, so complete in detail, so menacing in its intent, was but part of a world-plan to assure to Germany when the time was ripe the submission of all her enemies and the peaceful assistance and acquiescence in her aims of those parts of the world which at that time should be at peace. Germany looked far ahead on that day when she first knew that war must come. She realised, if no other nation did, that however strong in themselves the combatants were, the neutrals who should command the world's supplies would really determine the victory.

Knowing this, Germany—which does not play the game of diplomacy with gloves on—laid her plans accordingly.

The United States offered a peculiarly fruitful field for her endeavours. By tradition and geography divorced from European rivalries, it was,

Germany's Hate Campaign

nevertheless, from both an industrial and agricultural standpoint, obviously to become the most important of neutral nations. The United States alone could feed and equip a continent; and it needed no prophet to perceive that whichever country could appropriate to itself her resources would unquestionably win the war, if a speedy military victory were not forthcoming.

It was Germany's aim, therefore, to prepare the way by which she could secure those supplies, or, failing in that, to keep them from the enemy, England—if England it should be. In a military way such a plan had little chance of success. England's command of the seas was too complete for Germany to consider that she could establish a successful blockade against her. It was then, I fancy, that Germany bethought herself of a greatly potential ally in the millions of citizens of German birth or parentage with whom the United States was filled.

One may extract a trifle of cynical amusement from what followed. Those millions of German-Americans had never been regarded with affection in Berlin. The vast majority of them were descendants of men who had left their homes for political reasons; and of those who had been born in Germany many had emigrated to escape military ser-

Germany's Hate Campaign

vice, and others had gone to seek a better opportunity than their native land provided. They had been called renegades who had given up their true allegiance for citizenship in a foreign country, and Bernstorff himself, according to the evidence of U.S. Senator Phelan, had said that he regarded them as traitors and cowards.

But Germany voicing her own spleen in private, and Germany with an axe to grind, were two different entities. And no one who observed the honeyed beginnings of the Deutschtum movement in America would have believed that these men who in public life were so assiduously and graciously flattered were in private characterised as utter traitors to the Fatherland—and worse.

Certainly no one believed it when, in 1900, Prince Henry of Prussia paid his famous visit to America. No word of criticism of these " traitors " was spoken by him; and when at banquets glasses were raised and Milwaukee smiled across the table at Berlin, the sentimental onlooker might have felt a gush of joy at this spectacle of amity and reconciliation. And the sentimental onlooker would never have suspected that Prince Henry had travelled three thousand miles for any other purpose than to attend the launching of the

Germany's Hate Campaign

Kaiser's yacht *Meteor*, which was then building in an American yard.

But to the cynical observer, searching the records of the years immediately following Prince Henry's visit, a few strange facts would have become apparent. He would have discovered that German societies, which had been neither very numerous nor popular before, had in a comparatively short time acquired a membership and a prominence that were little short of marvellous. He would have noted the increasing number of German teachers and professors who appeared in the faculties of American schools and colleges. He would have remarked the growth in popularity of the German newspapers, many of them edited by Germans who had never become naturalised. And yet, observing these things, he might have agreed with the vast majority of Americans in regarding them as entirely harmless and of significance merely as a proof of how hard love of one's native land dies.

He would have been mistaken had he so regarded them. The German Government does not spend money for sentimental purposes; and in the last ten years that Government has expended literally millions of dollars for propaganda in the United States. It has consistently encouraged a

Germany's Hate Campaign

sentiment for the Fatherland that should be so strong that it would hold first place in the heart of every German-American. It has circulated pamphlets advocating the exclusive use of the German language, not merely in the homes, but in shops and street cars and all other public places. It has lent financial support to German organisations in America, and in a thousand ways has aimed so to win the hearts of the German-Americans that when the time should come the United States, by sheer force of numbers, would be delivered, bound hand and foot, into the hands of the German Government.

It was this object of undermining the true allegiance of the German citizens of the United States which transformed an innocent and natural tendency into a menace that was the more insidious because the very people involved were, for the most part, entirely ignorant of its true nature. Germany seized upon an attachment that was purely one of sentiment and race and sought to make it an instrument of political power; and she went about her work with so efficient a secrecy that she very nearly accomplished her purpose.

By the time the Great War broke out the German propaganda in America had assumed notable proportions. German newspapers were

Germany's Hate Campaign

plentiful and had acquired a tremendous influence over the minds of the German-speaking folk. Many of the German societies had been consolidated into one national organisation—the German-American National Alliance, with a membership of two millions, and a president, C. J. Hexamer, of Chicago, whose devotion to the Fatherland has been so great that he has been decorated with the Order of the Red Eagle. And the German people of the United States had, by a long campaign of flattery and cajolery, coupled with a systematic glorification of German genius and institutions, been won to attachment to the country of their origin that required only a touch to translate it into fanaticism.

Germany had set the stage and rehearsed the chorus. There were needed only the principals to make the drama complete. These she provided in the persons of four men: Franz von Papen, Karl Boy-Ed, Heinrich Albert, and later Franz von Rintelen.

They were no ordinary men whom Germany had appointed to the leadership of this giant underground warfare against a peaceful country. Highly bred, possessing a wide and intensive knowledge of finance, of military strategy and of diplomatic finesse, they were admirably equipped

Germany's Hate Campaign

to win the admiration and trust of the people of America at the very moment that they were attacking them. All of them were men skilled in the art of making friends; and so successfully did they employ this art that their popularity for a long time contrived to shield them from suspicion. Each of these men was assigned to the command of some particular branch of German secret service. And each brought to his task the resources of the scientist, the soldier and the statesman, coupled with the scruples of the bandit.

It is impossible in this brief space to tell the full story of the activities of these gentlemen and of their many highly trained assistants. Violence, as you know, played no small part in their plans. Sedition, strikes in munitions plants, attacks upon ships carrying supplies to the Allies, the crippling of transportation facilities, bomb outrages—these are a few of the main elements in the campaign to render the United States useless as a source of supply for Germany's enemies. But ultimately of more importance than this was a programme of publicity which should not only present to the German-Americans the viewpoint of their Fatherland (an entirely legitimate propaganda), but which was aimed to consolidate them into a political unit which should

Germany's Hate Campaign

be used, by peaceful means if possible—such as petitions and the like, but if that method failed, by *absolute armed resistance*—to force the United States Government to declare an embargo upon shipments of munitions and foodstuffs to the Allies, and to compel it to assume a position if not of active alliance with Germany (a hope that was never seriously entertained) at least one which should distinctly favour the German Government and cause serious dissension between America and England.

There followed a twofold campaign: on the one hand, active terrorism against private industry in so far as it was of value to the Allies, reinforced by the most determined plots against Canada; on the other, an insincere and lying propaganda that presented the United States Government as a pretender of a neutrality which it did not attempt to practise—as an institution controlled by men who were unworthy of the support of any but Anglophiles and hypocrites.

Left to itself, the sympathy of German-Americans would have been directed towards Germany; stimulated as it was by an unremitting campaign of publicity, this sympathy became a devotion almost rabid in its intensity. Race consciousness was aroused and placed upon the

Germany's Hate Campaign

defensive by the attitude of the larger portion of the American Press, and the German-Americans grew defiant and aggressive in their apologies for the Fatherland. Even those whose German origin was so remote that they were ignorant of the very language of their fathers, subscribed to newspapers and periodicals whose sole reason for existence was that they presented the truth—as Germany saw it. If in that presentation the German Press adopted a tone that was seditious —why, there were those in Berlin who would applaud the more heartily. And in New York Captain von Papen and his colleagues would read and nod their heads approvingly.

At the end of the first two months of the war, and of my active service in America, the campaign of violence was well under way. Already plans had been made for several enterprises other than the Welland Canal plot, about which you read in Chapter VII. Attacks had been planned against vulnerable points on the Canadian Pacific Railway, such as the St. Clair Tunnel running under the Detroit River at Point Huron, Michigan; agents had been planted in the various munitions factories, and spies were everywhere seeking possible points of vantage at which a blow for Germany could be struck. A plan had

Germany's Hate Campaign

even then been made to blow up the railway bridge at Vanceboro.

But already von Papen and his associates, including myself, knew that Germany could never succeed in crippling Allied commerce in the United States and in proceeding effectively against Canada until we could count upon the implicit co-operation of the German-Americans, even though that co-operation involved active disloyalty to the country of their adoption.

There lay the difficulty. That the bulk of the German-Americans were loyal to their Government I knew at the time. Now, happily, that is a matter which is beyond doubt. Among them there were, of course, many whose zeal outran their scruples and others whose scruples were for sale. But for the most part, although they could be cajoled into a partnership that was not always prudent, they could not be led beyond this point into positive defiance of the United States, however mistaken they might believe its policies.

The rest of the story I cannot tell at first hand, for I was not directly concerned in the events that followed. What I know I have pieced together from my recollection of conversations with von Papen, and from what many people in Berlin, who thought I was familiar with the affair, told

Germany's Hate Campaign

me. Who fathered the idea I do not know. Someone conceived a scheme so treacherous and contemptible that every other act of this war seems white beside it. *It was planned so to discredit the German-Americans that the hostility of their fellow-citizens would force them back into the arms of the German Government.* These millions of American citizens of German descent were to be given the appearance of disloyalty in order that they might become objects of suspicion to their fellows, and through their resentment at this attitude the cleavage between Germans and non-Germans in America would be increased and perhaps culminate in armed conflict.

On the face of it this looks like the absurd and impossible dream of an insane person rather than a diplomatic programme. And yet, if it be examined more closely, the plan will be seen to have a psychological basis which, however farfetched, is essentially sound. Given a people already bewildered by the almost universal condemnation of a country which they have sincerely revered; add to that serious difference in sympathies an attitude of distrust of all German-Americans by the other inhabitants of the country; and you have sown the seed of a race-antagonism

Germany's Hate Campaign

which if properly nurtured may easily grow into a violent hatred. In a word, Germany had decided that if the German-Americans could not be coaxed back into the fold they might be beaten back. She set about her part of the task with an industry which would have commanded admiration had it been better employed.

Glance back over the history of the past three years and consider how, almost overnight, the "hyphen" situation developed. America, shaken by a war which had been declared to be impossible, became suddenly conscious of the presence within her borders of a portion of her population—a nation in numbers—largely unassimilated, retaining its own language, and possessing characteristics which suddenly became conspicuously distasteful. Inevitably, as I say, the cleavage in sympathies produced distrust. But it was not until stories of plots in which German-Americans were implicated became current that this distrust developed into an acute suspicion. Germanophobia was rampant in those days, and to hysterical persons it was unthinkable that any German could be exempt from the suspicion of treason.

It was upon this foundation that the German agents erected their structure of lies and defama-

Germany's Hate Campaign

tion. Not content with the efforts which the Jingo Press and Jingo individuals were unconsciously making on their behalf, they deliberately set on foot rumours which were intended to increase the distrust of German-Americans. I happen to know that during the first two years of the War many of the stories about German attempts upon Canada, about German-American complicity in various plots, *emanated from the offices of Captain von Papen and his associates.* I know also that many plots in which German-Americans were concerned had been deliberately encouraged by von Papen and afterwards as deliberately betrayed! Time after time enterprises with no chance of success were set on foot with the sole purpose that they should fail—for thus Germany could furnish to the world evidence that America was honeycombed with sedition and treachery—evidence which Americans themselves would be the first to accept.

It was in reality a gigantic game of bluff. Germany wished to give to the world convincing proof that all peoples of German descent were solidly supporting her. It was for this reason that reports of impossible German activities were set afloat; that rumours of Germans massing in the Maine woods, of aeroplane flights over

Germany's Hate Campaign

Canada, and of all sorts of enterprises which had no basis in fact, were disseminated. And since many anti-German papers had been indiscreet enough to attack the German-Americans as disloyal, the German agents used and fomented these attacks for their own purposes.

Who could gain by such a campaign of slander and the feeling it would produce? Certainly not the Administration, which had great need of a united country behind it. Certainly not the American Press, which was bound to lose circulation and advertising; nor American business, which would suffer from the loss of thousands of customers of German descent, who would turn to the German merchant for their needs. Only two classes could profit: the German Press, which was liberally subsidised by the German Government, and the German Government itself.

It was to the interests of the Administration at Washington to keep the country united by keeping the Germans disunited. The reverse condition would tend to indicate that Americanism was a failure, since the country was divided at a critical time; it would seriously hamper the Government in its dealings with all the warring nations; and it would be of benefit only to the German societies and German Press, and through

Germany's Hate Campaign

them to the German Government. It *was* of benefit. The German newspapers increased their circulations and advertising revenues, in many cases by more than 100 per cent. German banks and insurance companies received money which had formerly gone to American institutions, and which now went to swell the Imperial German War Loans. And the German clubs increased their memberships and became more and more instruments of power in the work of Germany.

There is a typical German Club in New York —the Deutscher Verein in Central Park South. During the war it has been used as a sub-office of the German General Staff. It was here that von Papen used to store the dynamite that was needed in such enterprises as the Welland Canal plot. It was here that conspirators used to meet for conferences which no one, not even the other members of the Club, could tell were not as innocent as they seemed.

These German societies and other agencies were used not merely to promote sympathy for the German cause, but also to influence public opinion in matters of purely American interest. On January 21, 1916, Henry Weismann, president of the Brooklyn branch of the German-American National Alliance, sent a report to

Germany's Hate Campaign

headquarters in Chicago regarding the activities of his organisation in the recent elections. In the Twenty-third Congressional District of New York, Ellsworth J. Healey had been a candidate for Congress. Both he and another man, John J. Fitzgerald, candidate for Justice of the Supreme Court of New York, were regarded by German interests as "unneutral." They were defeated, and Weismann, in commenting upon the matter, wrote: "*The election returns prove that Deutschtum is armed and able, when the word is given, to seat its men.*"

Even in the campaign for preparedness Germany took a hand. Berlin was appealed to in some cases as to the attitude that American citizens of German descent should adopt towards this policy. Professor Appelmann, of the University of Vermont, wrote to Dr. Paul Rohrbach, one of the advisers of the Wilhelmstrasse, requesting his advice upon the subject. Dr. Rohrbach replied that American Deutschtum should not be in favour of preparedness, because "*it is quite conceivable that in the event of an American-Japanese war, Germany might adopt an attitude of very benevolent neutrality towards Japan and so make it easier for Japan to defeat the United States.*" And not long ago the *Herold des Glaubens* of St.

Germany's Hate Campaign

Louis made this statement: " When we found that the agitation for preparedness was in the interest of the munition makers, and that its aim was a war with Germany, we certainly turned against it, and we have agitated against it for the last three months."

But this anti-militaristic spirit was a rather sudden development on the part of the German societies. In 1911, when a new treaty of arbitration with Great Britain was under consideration, a group of roughs, *led and organised by a German,* violently broke up a meeting held under the auspices of the New York Peace Society to support that treaty. The man who broke that meeting up was Alphonse G. Koelble. It was this same Koelble who in 1915, when Germany's attack upon America was most bitter, organised a meeting of " The Friends of Peace," in order to protest against militarism! Strange, is it not, this inconsistency? *Or was it that Mr. Koelble was acting under orders ?*

Germany did these things not only for their political effect, but also because she knew that she could turn the evidence of her own meddling to account. It was for the same reason that Wolf von Igel, von Papen's secretary and successor, retained in his office a list of American citizens

Germany's Hate Campaign

of German descent who "could be relied on." This list was found by agents of the Department of Justice when von Igel's office was raided. And the German agents were glad it was discovered. *It gave to Americans an additional proof of the hold which Germany had obtained over a large group of German-Americans.*

It was as late as March, 1916, that the members of the Minnesota Chapter of the German-American National Alliance received a circular, advising them of the attitude *towards Germany* of the various candidates for delegate to the national conventions of the different parties, and indicating by a star the names of those men "about whom it has been ascertained that they are in agreement with the views and wishes of Deutschland, and that if elected they will act accordingly." I do not believe that the men who sent that circular expected it to be widely obeyed. But unquestionably they knew it would be made public.

I think that if the German conspirators in America had confined their activities to this field they might ultimately have succeeded. They had managed to seduce a sufficient number of German-Americans to cause the entire German-American population to be regarded with sus-

Germany's Hate Campaign

picion. They had contrived to discredit the Pacifist and Labour movements by making public their own connection with individuals in these bodies. They had aroused the public to such a pitch of distrust that in the Presidential campaign of 1916 the support of the "German vote" was regarded with distaste by both candidates. And they had helped to create so tremendous a dissension in America that friendships of long standing were broken up, German merchants in many communities lost all but their German customers, and German-Americans were belaboured in print with such twaddle as the following:

"The German-Americans predominate in the grog-shops, low dives, pawnshops and numerous artifices for money-making and corrupt practices in politics."

The foregoing statement, which I quote from a book, "German Conspiracies in the United States," is not perhaps a fair sample of the attacks made upon German-Americans by the Press in general, but it is indicative of the heights to which feeling ran in the case of a few uninformed or hysterical persons. The point is that to a large portion of the populace the German-Americans had become enemies and objects of abuse.

Germany's Hate Campaign

They, in turn, beset on all sides by a campaign of slander insidiously fostered by men to whom they had given their trust, did exactly what had been expected. They fell right into the arms of that movement which for fourteen years had been subsidised for that very purpose. They ceased to read American newspapers. They read German newspapers, many of which almost openly preached disloyalty to the United States. They became clannish and joined German societies which frequently contained German agents. They began to boycott American business houses and dealt only with those of German affiliation.

Germany had gained her point. She alone could gain by the disunion of the country. It was to her advantage that the profits which had formerly gone to American business houses should be deflected to German corporations. *And had she rested her efforts there, she might, as I say, have seen them produce results in the form of riots and armed dissension which would have effectually prevented the United States from entering the war.*

But Germany overreached herself. Emboldened by the apparent success of their schemes, her principal agents, von Papen, Boy-Ed and von

Germany's Hate Campaign

Rintelen (who had begun his work in January, 1915) became careless, so far as secrecy was concerned, and so audacious in their plans that they betrayed themselves, perhaps intentionally, as a final demonstration of their power. The results are notorious. In so far as the disclosures of their activities tended further to implicate the German-Americans, they did harm. But by these very disclosures the eyes of many German-Americans were opened to the true nature of the influence to which they had been subjected, and through that fact the worst element of the German propaganda in America received its death-blow.

To-day the United States is at war, and no intelligent man now questions the loyalty of the majority of the citizens of German blood. That in the past their sympathies have been with Germany is unquestioned and, from their standpoint, entirely proper. That in many cases they view the participation of the United States in the war with regret is probable. But that they will stand up and, if need be, fight as stanchly as any other group in the country, no man may doubt.

That is the story of the darkest chapter in the history of German intrigue. Other things have been done in this war at which a humane man

Germany's Hate Campaign

may blush. Other crimes have been committed which not even the strongest partisan can condone. But at least it may be said that these things were done to enemies or to neutral people whom fortune had put in the way of injury. The betrayal of the German-Americans was a wanton crime against men whom every association and every tie of kinship or tradition should have served to protect.

Germany has not yet abandoned that attack. There are still spies in the United States, you may be sure—still intrigues are being fostered. And there are still men who, consciously or unconsciously, are striving to discredit the German-Americans by presenting them as unwilling to bear their share in the burden of the nation's war. Only a week before these lines were written one man—George Sylvester Viereck—circulated a petition begging that Germans should not be sent to fight their countrymen, and an organisation of German Protestant churches in America repeated this plea. As a German whom fortune has placed outside the battle, and as one whose patriotism is extended towards blood rather than dynasty, I ask Mr. Viereck and these other gentlemen if they have not forgotten that many German-Americans have already shown their

Germany's Hate Campaign

feelings by volunteering for service in this war—and if they have not also forgotten that the two great wars of American history were fought between men of the same blood.

Ties of blood have never prevented men from fighting for a cause which they believed to be just. They will not in this war! And when Mr. Viereck and his kind protest against the participation in the war of men of any descent whatever, they imply that the American cause is *not* just, and that it is not worthy of the support of the men they claim to represent.

Is this their intention?

CHAPTER XI

MISCHIEF IN MEXICO

More about the German intrigue against the United States—German aims in Latin America—Japan and Germany in Mexico—What happened in Cuba?

"AMERICAN intervention in Mexico would mean another Ireland, another Poland—another sore spot in the world. Well, why not?"

Those were almost the last words spoken to me when I left Germany in 1914 upon my ill-fated mission to England. I had in my pocket at the moment detailed memoranda of instructions which, if they could be carried out, would insure such disturbances in Mexico that the United States would be compelled to intervene. I had been given authority to spend almost unlimited sums of money for the purchase of arms, for the bribery of officials—for anything, in fact, that would cause trouble in Mexico. And the words I have quoted were not spoken by an uninformed person with a taste for cynical comment; they were uttered by Major Köhnemann, of Abteilung

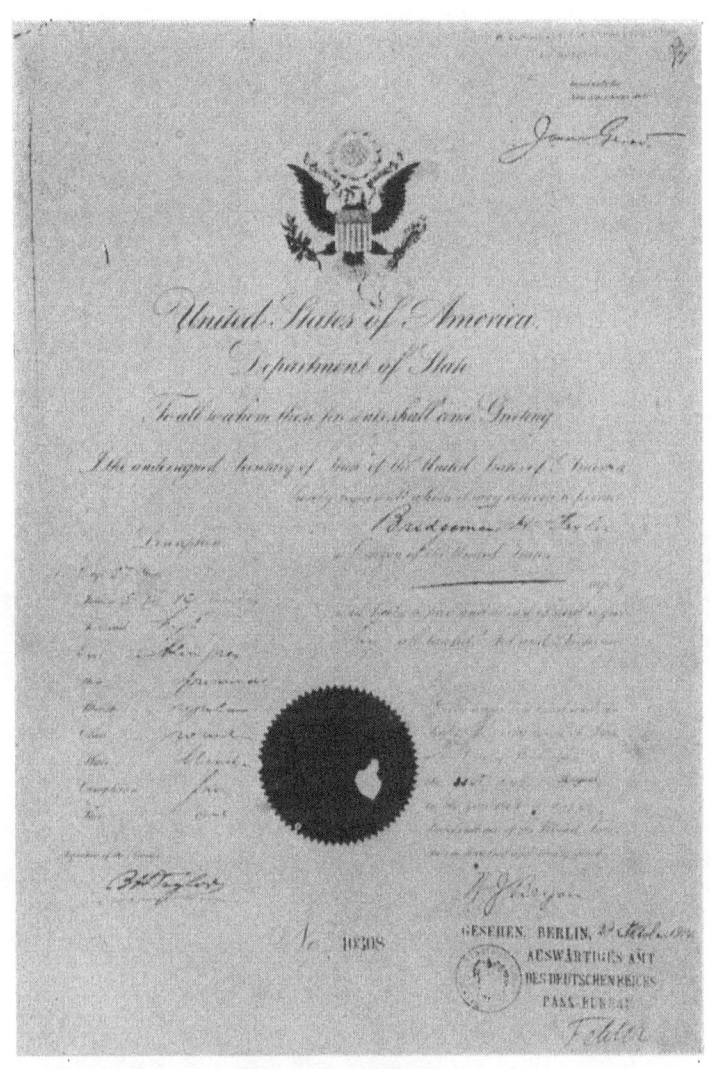

THE PASSPORT ON WHICH CAPTAIN VON DER GOLTZ WENT TO GERMANY AND ENGLAND. *(See p. 180)*
(Note the visé of the American Embassy, Berlin, in the top right-hand corner.)

SAFE-DEPOSIT RECEIPT FOR PAPERS WHICH CAPTAIN
VON DER GOLTZ LEFT IN ROTTERDAM. *(See p. 131)*

Mischief in Mexico

III. B of the German General Staff. They form a lucid and concrete explanation of German activities in Mexico during the past eight years.

Long before this war began German agents were at work in Mexico stirring up trouble in the hope of causing the United States to intervene. I have already told how, in 1910 and 1911, Germany had encouraged Japan and Mexico in negotiating a treaty that was to give Japan an important foothold in Mexico. I have told how, after this treaty was well on the way to completion, Germany saw to it that knowledge of the projected terms was brought to the attention of the United States—thereby indirectly causing Diaz's abdication (*see* Chapter V.). That instance is not an isolated case of German meddling in Mexican affairs. Rather is it symptomatic of the traditional policy of Wilhelmstrasse in regard to America.

It may be well to examine this policy more closely than I have done. Long ago Germany saw in South America a fertile field for exploitation, not only in a commercial way, in which it presented excellent opportunities to German manufacturers, but also as a possible opportunity for expansion which had been denied her elsewhere. All of the German colonies were in torrid

Mischief in Mexico

climates, in which life for the white man was attended with tremendous hardships, and exploitation and colonisation were consequently impeded. Only in the Far East and in South America could she find territories either unprotected through their own weakness, or so thinly settled that they offered at once a temptation and an opportunity to the nation with imperialistic ambitions. In the former quarters she was blocked by a concert of the Powers, many of them actuated by similar aims, but all working at such cross-purposes that aggression by any one of them was impossible. In Chapter II. I alluded to the result of such a situation in my discussion of the Anglo-Persian Agreement. In South America there was only one formidable obstacle to German expansion—the Monroe Doctrine.

I am stating the case with far less than its real complexity. There were, it is true, many facts in the form of conflicting rivalries of the Powers as well as internal conditions in South America, that would have had a deterrent effect upon the German programme. Nevertheless, it is certain that the prime factor in keeping Germany out of South America was the traditional policy of the United States; and, so far as the German Government's attitude in the matter is concerned,

Mischief in Mexico

it is the only phase of the problem worth considering.

Germany had no intention of securing territory by a war of conquest. Her method was far simpler and much less assailable. She promptly instituted a peaceful invasion of various parts of the continent; first, in the persons of merchants who captured trade but did not settle permanently in the country; second, by means of a vast army of immigrants, who, unlike those who a generation before had come to the United States, settled, *but retained their German citizenship.* With this unnaturalised element she hoped to form a nucleus in many of the important South American countries which, wielding a tremendous commercial power and possessing a political influence that was considerable, although indirect, would aid her in determining the course of South American politics, so that by a form of peaceful expansion she could eventually achieve her aims.

Was this a dream? At any rate, it received the support of many of the ablest statesmen of Gemany, who duly set about the task of discrediting the Monroe Doctrine in the eyes of the very people it was designed to protect, so that the United States, if it ever came forcibly to de-

Mischief in Mexico

fend the Doctrine, would find itself opposed not only by Germany, but by South America as well.

Now, the easiest way to cast suspicion upon a policy is to discredit the sponsor of it. In the case of the United States and South America this was not at all difficult; for the Southern nations already possessed a well-defined fear and a dislike of their northern neighbour which were not by any means confined to the more ignorant portions of the population. Fear of American aggression has been somewhat of a bugaboo in many quarters. Recognising this, Germany, which has always adopted the policy of aggravating ready-made troubles for her own ends, steadily fomented that fear by means of a quiet but well-conducted propaganda, *and also by seeking to force the United States into taking action that would justify that fear.*

As a means towards securing this latter end, Mexico presented itself as a heaven-sent opportunity. Even in the days when it was, to outward eyes, a well-ordered community, there had been men in the United States who had expressed themselves in favour of an expansion southwards which would result in the ultimate absorption of Mexico; and although such talk had never attracted much attention in the quarter from which it

Mischief in Mexico

emanated, there were those who saw to it that proposals of this sort received an effective publicity south of the Isthmus. Given, then, a Mexico in which discontent had become so acute that it was being regarded with alarm by American and foreign investors, the possibility of intervention became more immediate and the opportunity of the trouble-maker increased proportionately.

Germany's first step in this direction was the encouragement of a Japanese-Mexican alliance, the failure of which was a vital part of her programme. It was a risky undertaking, for if, by any chance, the alliance were successfully concluded, the United States might well hesitate to attack the combined forces of the two countries; and Mexico, fortified by Japan, would present a bulwark against the real or fancied danger of American expansion, that, for a time at least, would effectually allay the fears of South America. That risk Germany took and, in so far as she had planned to prevent the alliance, scored a success. That she failed in her principal aim was due to the anti-imperialist tendencies of the United States and the statesmanship of Señor Limantour rather than to any other cause.

Then came the Madero Administration with

Mischief in Mexico

its mystical programme of reform—and an opposition headed by almost all of the able men in the Republic, both Mexican and foreign. Bitterly fought by the ring of Científicos, who saw the easy spoils of the past slipping from their hands; distrusted by many honest men, who sincerely believed that Mexico was better ruled by an able despot than by an upright visionary; hampered by the aloofness of foreign business and Governments, waiting for a success which they alone could ensure, before they should approve and support; and constantly beset with uneasiness by the incomprehensible attitude of the Taft Administration and of its Ambassador—the fate of the Madero Government was easily foreseen.

Before Madero had been in power for three months this opposition had taken form as a campaign of obstruction in the Mexican Chamber of Deputies supported by the Press, controlled almost exclusively by the Científicos and by foreign capitalists; by the clergy, who had reason to suspect the Government of anti-clerical tendencies; and by isolated groups of opportunity-seekers who saw in the Administration an obstacle to their own political and economic aims. The Madero family were represented as incompetent and self-seeking; and in a short time the populace, which

Mischief in Mexico

a month before had hailed the new Government as a saviour of the country, had been persuaded that its programme of economic reform had been merely a political pretence, and accordingly added its strength to the party of the Opposition.

Here was tinder in plenty for a conflagration of sorts. Germany applied the torch at its most inflammable spot.

That inflammable spot happened to be a man —Pazcual Orozco. Orozco had been one of Madero's original supporters, and in the days of the Madero revolution had rendered valuable services to his chief. An ex-muleteer, uncouth and without education, he possessed considerable ability; but his vanity and reputation were far in excess of his attainments. Unquestionably he had expected that Madero's success would mean a brilliant future for himself, although it is difficult to tell in just what direction his ambitions pointed. Madero had placed him in command of the most important division of the Federal army, but this presumably did not content him. At any rate, early in February, 1912, he made a demand upon the Government for two hundred and fifty thousand pesos, threatening that he would withdraw from the services of the Government unless this " honorarium "—honesty would call it a bribe

Mischief in Mexico

—were paid to him. Madero refused his demand, but with mistaken leniency retained Orozco in office—and on February 27, Orozco repaid this trust by turning traitor at Chihuahua, and involving in his defection six thousand of Mexico's best troops as well as a quantity of supplies.

Now mark the trail of German intrigue. In Mexico City, warmly supporting the Madero Government, but of little real power in the country, was the German Minister, Admiral von Hintze. In normal circumstances, his influence would have been of great value in helping to render secure the position of Madero; but with means of communication disrupted as they were to a large extent, his power was inconceivably smaller than that of the German Consuls, all of whom were well liked and respected by the Mexicans with whom they were in close touch. Apart from their political office, these men represented German business interests in Mexico, particularly in the fields of hardware and banking. In the three northern cities of Parral, Chihuahua and Zacatecas, the German Consuls were hardware merchants. In Torreon the Consul was director of the German bank. As such it would seem that it was to their interests to work for the preservation of a stable government in Mexico. And yet the fact remains

Mischief in Mexico

that when Orozco first began to show signs of discontent, these men encouraged him with a support that was both moral and financial; and when the general finally turned traitor, it was my old friend, Consul Kueck, who, as President of the Chamber of Commerce of Chihuahua, voted to support him and to recognise Orozco's supremacy in that State!

I leave it to the reader to decide whether it was the Minister or the Consuls who really represented the German Government.

It would be idle to attempt to trace more than in the briefest way Germany's part in the events of the next few years. Always she followed a policy of obstruction and deceit. During the months immediately succeeding the Orozco outbreak, at the very moment that von Hintze was lending his every effort to the preservation of the Madero régime, sending to Berlin reports which over and over again reiterated his belief that Madero could, if given a free hand, restore order in the Republic, the German Consuls were openly fomenting disorder in the north.

They were particularly well equipped to make trouble, by their position in the community and by the character and reputation of the rest of the German population. It may be said with safety that

Mischief in Mexico

however careless Germany has been about the quality of the men whom she has allowed to emigrate to other countries, her representatives throughout all of Latin-America have been conspicuous for their commercial attainments and for their social adaptability. This, in a large way, has been responsible for the German commercial success in Central and South America. As bankers they have been honest and obliging in the matter of credit. As merchants they have adapted themselves to the local conditions and to the habits of their customers with notable success. In consequence they have been well liked as individuals and have been of immense value in increasing the prestige of the German Empire. In Mexico they were the only foreigners who were not disliked by either peon or aristocrat; and it is significant to note that during seven years of unrest in that country, Germans alone among peoples of European stock have remained practically unmolested by any party.

Consider of what service this condition was in their campaign. Respected and influential, they were in an excellent position to stimulate whatever anti-American feeling existed in Latin American countries. At the same time, they were equally well situated to encourage the unrest in

Mischief in Mexico

Mexico that would be the surest guarantee of American intervention—and the coalition against the United States which intervention would be certain to provoke. They made the utmost use of their advantage, and they did it without arousing suspicion or rebuke.

After the failure of the short-lived Orozco outbreak, events in Mexico seemed to promise a peaceful solution of all difficulties. Many of Madero's opponents declared a truce, and the irreconcilables were forced to bide their time in apparent harmlessness. In November came the rebellion of Felix Diaz, fathered by a miscellaneous group of conspirators who hoped to find in the nephew sufficient of the characteristics of the great Porfirio to serve their purposes. This venture failed also. Again Madero showed a mistaken leniency in preserving the life of Diaz. He paid for it with his life. Out of this uprising came the *coup d'état* of General Huerta—made possible by a dual treachery—and the murder of the only man who at the time gave promise of eventually solving the Mexican problem.

What share German agents had in that tragic affair I do not know. You may be sure that they took advantage of any opportunity that presented itself to encourage the conspirators in a project

Mischief in Mexico

that gave such rich promise of aiding them in their purposes. I pass on to the next positive step in their campaign. That was a repetition of their old plan of inserting the Japanese question into the general muddle.

The Japanese question in Mexico is a very real one. I know—and the United States Government presumably knows, also—that Japan is the only nation which has succeeded in gaining a permanent foothold in Mexico. I know that spies and secret agents in the guise of pedlars, engineers, fishermen, farmers, charcoal-burners, merchants, and even officers in the armies of every Mexican leader have been scattered throughout the country. The number of these latter I have heard estimated at about eight hundred; at any rate it is considerable. There are also about ten thousand Japanese who have no direct connection with Tokio, but who are practically all men of military age, either unmarried or without wives in Mexico—most of them belonging to the army or navy reserve. And, like the Germans, the Japanese never lose their connection with the Government in their capacity as private individuals.

Through the great Government-owned steamship line, the Toyo Kisen Kaisha, the Japanese Government controls the land for a Japanese coal-

Mischief in Mexico

ing station at Manzanillo. At Acapulco a Japanese company holds a land concession on a high hill three miles from the sea. It is difficult to see what legitimate use a fishing company could make of this location. It is, however, an ideal site for a wireless station. In Mexico City an intimate friend of the Japanese Chargé d'Affaires owns a fortress-like building in the very heart of the capital. Another Japanese holds, under a ninety-nine years' lease, an L-shaped strip of land partly surrounding and completely commanding the waterworks of the capital of Oxichimilco. The land is undeveloped. Both of these Japanese are well supplied with money and have been living in Mexico City for several years. Neither has any visible means of support. And in all of the years of revolution in Mexico no Japanese has been killed—except by Villa. He has caused many of them to be executed, but always those that were masquerading as Chinese. Naturally a Government cannot protest in such circumstances.

These facts may or may not be significant. They serve to lend colour to the convictions of anti-Japanese agitators in the United States, and as such they have been of value to Germany. Accordingly it was suggested to Señor Huerta

Mischief in Mexico

that an alliance with Japan would be an excellent protective measure for him to take.

Huerta had two reasons for looking with favour upon this proposal. He was very decidedly in the bad graces of Washington, and he was constantly menaced by the presence in Mexico of Felix Diaz, to whom he had agreed to resign the Presidency. Diaz was too popular to be shot, too strong politically to be exiled, and yet—he must be removed. Here, thought Huerta, was an opportunity of killing two birds with one stone. He therefore sent Diaz to Japan, ostensibly to thank the Japanese Government for its participation in the Mexican Centennial celebration, three years before, but in reality to begin negotiations for a treaty which should follow the lines of one unsuccessfully promulgated in 1911.

Señor Diaz started for Japan—but he never arrived there. Somehow the State Department at Washington got news of the proposed treaty—how, only the German agents know—and Señor Diaz's course was diverted.

Meanwhile, in spite of the strained relations between Huerta and Washington, Germany was aiding the Mexican President with money and supplies. In the north, Consuls Kueck of Chihuahua, Sommer of Durango, Müller of Her-

Mischief in Mexico

mosillo, and Weber of Juarez were exhibiting the same interest in the Huertista troops that they had formerly displayed towards Orozco. Kueck, as I happened to learn later, had financed Salvator Mercado, the general who had so obligingly tried to have me shot; and at the same time he was assiduously spreading reports of unrest in Mexico, and even attempted to bribe some Germans to leave the country, upon the plea that their lives were in danger.

When I raided the German Consulate at Chihuahua, I found striking documentary proof of his activities in this direction. There were letters there proving that he had paid to various Germans sums ranging as high as fifty dollars a month, upon condition that they should remain outside of Mexico. These letters, in many cases, showed plainly that this was done in order to make it seem that the unrest was endangering the lives of foreign inhabitants, in spite of which several of the recipients complained that their absence from Mexico was causing them considerable financial loss, and showed an evident desire to brave whatever dangers there might be—if they could secure the permission of Consul Kueck.

During the year and more that Huerta held power, Germany followed the same tactics. I need

Mischief in Mexico

not mention the attempt to supply Huerta with munitions after the United States had declared an embargo upon them; or that it has been generally admitted that the real purpose of the seizure of Vera Cruz by United States marines was to prevent the German steamer *Ypiranga* from delivering her cargo of arms to the Mexicans. That is but one instance of the way in which German policy worked —a policy which, as I have indicated, was opposed to the true interests of Mexico, and has been solely directed against the United States. Up to the very outbreak of the war it continued. After Villa's breach with Carranza, emissaries of Consul Kueck approached the former with offers of assistance. Strangely enough, he rejected them, principally because he hates the Germans for the assistance they gave his old enemy, Orozco. Villa had, moreover, a personal grudge against Kueck. When General Mercado was defeated at Ojinaga, papers were found in his effects that implicated the Consul in a conspiracy against the Constitutionalists, although at the time Kueck professed friendship for Villa and was secretly doing all he could to increase the friction that existed between the general and Mercado. Villa had sworn vengeance against the double-dealer; and Kueck, in alarm, fled into the United States.

[Copy.]

No. 1.

ALIENS RESTRICTION ACT, 1914.

ORDER for the DEPORTATION of

Horst Von der Goltz,

an Alien.

IN PURSUANCE of the powers conferred by the Aliens Restriction Act, 1914, and of Article XII of the Order in Council made under that Act on the 9th September, 1914, I HEREBY ORDER that

Horst Von der Goltz

an Alien, shall be deported from the United Kingdom.

DONE at Whitehall this 9th day of April, 1915.

(Signed) R. McKenna,

One of His Majesty's Principal Secretaries of State.

THE ORDER FOR THE DEPORTATION OF CAPTAIN VON DER GOLTZ FROM THE UNITED KINGDOM.

(*See p.* 133)

Mischief in Mexico

With the outbreak of the Great War the situation changed in one important particular. Heretofore, German activities had been part of a plan of attack upon the prestige of the United States. Now they became necessary as a measure of defence. Before two months had passed it became evident to the German Government that the United States *must* be forced into a war with Mexico in order to prevent the shipment of munitions to Europe.

So began the last stage of the German intrigue in Mexico—an intrigue which still continues. As a preliminary step, Germany had organised her own citizens in that country into a well-drilled military unit—a little matter which Captain von Papen had attended to during the spring of 1914. One can read much between the lines of the report sent to the Imperial Chancellor by Admiral von Hintze, commenting upon the work of Captain von Papen in this direction. The admiral says in part:

"He showed especial industry in organising the Germany colony for purposes of self-defence, and out of this shy and factious material, unwilling to undertake any military activity, he obtained what there was to be got."

Von Hintze significantly recommends that the

Mischief in Mexico

captain should be decorated with the fourth class of the Order of the Red Eagle.

As related in Chapter IX., I left Germany in October of 1914 with a detailed plan of campaign for the "American front," as Dr. Albert once put it. My final instructions were simple and explicit.

"There must be constant uprisings in Mexico," I was told in effect. "Villa, Carranza, must be reached. Zapata must continue his maraudings. It does not matter in the least how you produce these results. Merely produce them. All Consuls have been instructed to furnish you with whatever sums you need—*and they will not ask you any questions.*"

Rather complete, was it not? I left with every intention of carrying the instructions out—and in a little over a week was made *hors de combat*. It was then that von Rintelen, who had already planned to come over to the United States in order to inaugurate a vast blockade-running system, undertook to add my undertaking to his own responsibilities.

What von Rintelen did is well known, so I shall only summarise it here. His first act was an attempted restitution of General Huerta, which he knew was the most certain method of causing intervention. Into this enterprise both Boy-Ed and

Mischief in Mexico

von Papen were impressed, and the three men set about the task of making arrangements with former Huertistas for a new uprising to be financed by German money. They sent agents to Barcelona to persuade the former Dictator to enter into the scheme; and finally, when the General was on his way to America, they attempted to arrange it so that he should arrive safely in New York and ultimately in Mexico. It was a plan remarkably well conceived and well executed. It would have succeeded but for one thing. General Huerta was captured by the United States authorities at the very moment that he tried to cross from Texas into Mexico!

But the indomitable von Rintelen was not discouraged. He had but one purpose—to make trouble—and he made it with a will. He sent money to Villa, and then, like the philanthropist in Chesterton's play, supported the other side by aiding Carranza, financing Zapata and starting two other revolutions in Mexico. Meanwhile anti-American feeling continued to be stirred up. German papers in Mexico presented the Fatherland's case as eloquently as they did elsewhere, and to a far more appreciative audience. Carranza was encouraged in his rather unfriendly attitude towards Washington. In a word, no step was

Mischief in Mexico

neglected which would embarrass the Wilson Administration and make peace between the two countries less certain or more difficult to maintain.

Need I complete the story? Is it necessary to tell how, after the recall of von Papen and Boy-Ed and the escape of von Rintelen, Mexico continued to be used as the catspaw of the German plotters? Everyone knows the events of the last few months; of the concentration of German reservists in various parts of Mexico; of the bitter attacks made upon the United States by pro-German newspapers; and of the reports, greatly exaggerating German activities in Mexico, which have been circulated with the direct intention of provoking still more ill-feeling between the two countries by leading Americans to believe that Mexico is honeycombed with German conspiracies.

These activities have not applied to Mexico alone. It is significant that twice in February of 1917 the Venezuelan Government has declined to approve of the request of President Wilson that other neutral nations should join him in breaking diplomatic relations with Germany as a protest against submarine warfare, and that many Venezuelan papers have stated that this refusal is due to the representations of resident Germans, who are many and influential. These are, of course,

Mischief in Mexico

legitimate activities, but they are in every case attended by a threat. Revolutions are easily begun in Latin America, and the obstinate Government can always be brought to a reasonable viewpoint by the example of recent uprisings or revolutions, financed by Germany, in Costa Rica, Peru and Cuba. Within a very recent time rumours were afloat in Venezuela that Germany had assisted General Cipriano Castro in the revolutionary movement that he had been organising in Porto Rico. It was reported that there were on the Colombian frontier many disaffected persons who would gladly join Castro if he landed in Colombia and marched on Carácas, as he did successfully in 1890.

For several years the Telefunken Company, a German corporation, has tried to obtain from the Venezuelan Government a concession to operate a wireless plant, which should be of greater power than any other in South America. When this proposal was last made certain Ministers were for accepting it, but the majority of the Government realised the uses to which the plant could be put and refused to grant the concession. An alternative proposal, made by the Government, to establish a station of less strength was rejected by the Company.

Mischief in Mexico

Germany has steadily sought such wireless sites throughout this region. Several have been established in Mexico, and in 1914 it was through a wireless station in Colombia that the German Admiral von Spee was enabled to keep himself informed of the movements of the squadron of Admiral Sir Christopher Cradock—information which resulted in the naval battle in Chilean waters with a loss of three British battleships. It was after this battle that Colombia ordered the closing of all wireless stations on its coasts.

In Cuba, too, the hand of Germany has been evident, in spite of the disclaimers which were made by both parties in the rebellion which, in 1916, grew out of the contested election in which both President Menocal and the Liberal candidate, Alfredo Zayas, claimed a victory. It is strange, if this were the real cause of the uprising, that hostilities did not start until 9th February, 1917, when General Gómez, himself an ex-President, began a revolt in the eastern portion of the island. The date is important; it was barely a week before new elections were to be held in two disputed provinces and *only six days after the United States had severed diplomatic relations with the German Government, and but four days after President Menocal's Government had de-*

Mischief in Mexico

clared its intention of following the action of the United States.

A little study of the personnel and developments of the rebellion furnishes convincing evidence as to its true backing. The Liberal Party is strongly supported by the Spanish element of the population, which is almost unanimously pro-German in its sympathies. All over the island, both Germans and Spaniards were arrested for complicity in the uprising. Nor have the clergy escaped. Literally, dozens of bishops were imprisoned in Havana upon the same charges.

It is also a notorious fact that the Mexicans have supported the Liberals, and that the staffs of the Liberal newspapers are almost exclusively composed of Mexican journalists. These newspapers were suppressed at the beginning of the revolution.

But far more significant are the developments in the actual fighting.

Most of the action has taken place in the eastern provinces of Camaguey, Oriente and Santa Clara—in which the more fertile fields of sugar cane are situated. The damage to the cane fields has been estimated at 5,000,000 tons and is, *from a military standpoint, unnecessary.*

Colonel Rigoberto Fernández, one of the revo-

Mischief in Mexico

lutionary leaders, stated that the rebels were plentifully supplied with hand grenades and artillery—although the reports prove that they had none. Was this an empty boast—or may there be a connection between Fernandez's statement and the capture by the British of three German ships, which were found off the Azores, laden with mines and arms?

I was in Havana in the latter part of March —upon a private errand, although the Cuban papers persisted in imputing sinister designs to me. Naturally, the Germans were not inclined to tell all their secrets, but my Mexican acquaintances, all of whom were well informed regarding Cuban affairs, gave me considerable information. Among other Mexicans I met General Joaquin Maas, the former General of the Federal forces under Huerta. The General has since made peace with Carranza and was at this time acting as the latter's go-between in negotiations with Germany. When I last saw Maas it was after the battle of El Paredo. He was about to blow out his brains, but one of his lieutenants elegantly informed him that he was a fool and dissuaded him from suicide. Maas received me with the courtesy due to a former opponent, and was not averse from telling me much about the situation. I also had

Mischief in Mexico

ample occasion to speak with Spaniards, whose sympathies were decidedly pro-German.

Little by little I was enabled to acquire a rather complete idea—not of the issues underlying the Cuban revolution, but of what had brought matters to a head. The answer may be found in one word—Germany. German agents—notably Dr. Hawe ben Hawas, who took a mysterious botanising expedition throughout that part of Cuba which later became the scene of revolutionary activities, and who has thrice been arrested as a German spy—saw in the political unrest of the country another opportunity to create a diversion in favour of Germany. Cuba at peace was a valuable economic ally of the United States. Cuba in rebellion was a source of annoyance to the country, since it meant intervention, the political value of which was unfavourable to the United States, and a serious loss in sugar, which is one of the most important ingredients in the manufacture of several high explosives.

Hence the burning of millions of tons of sugar cane. Hence the rebel seizure of Santiago de Cuba. Hence the large number of negroes who joined the rebel army, and whose labour is indispensable in the production of sugar.

The ironic part of it all is that Germany had

Mischief in Mexico

nothing to gain by a change of government in Cuba. Any Cuban Government must have a sympathetic attitude towards the United States. What Germany wanted was a disruption of the orderly life of the country—and she wanted it to continue for as long a time as possible.

At the present writing the Cuban rebellion is ended. General Gómez and his army have been captured, President Menocal is firmly seated in power again, and the rebels hold only a few unimportant points. But much damage has been done in the lessening of the sugar supply—and the rebellion has also served its purpose as an illustration of Germany's ability to make trouble.

Germany has played a consistent game throughout. She has sought to use all the existing weaknesses of the world for her own purposes—all the rivalries, all the fears, all the antipathies, she has utilised as fuel for her own fire. And yet, although she has played the game with the utmost foresight, with a skill that is admirable in spite of its perverse uses, and with an unfailing assurance of success—she has come to the fourth year of the Great War with the fact of failure staring her in the face.

But she has not given up. You may be sure that she has not given up.

CHAPTER XII

THE COMPLETE SPY

The last stand of German intrigue—Germany's spy system in America.—What is coming?

As I write these last few pages three clippings from recent newspapers lie before me on my desk. One of them tells of the new era of good feeling that exists between the Governments of Mexico and the United States, and speaks of the alliance of Latin American Republics against German autocracy.

Another tells how the first contingent of American troops has landed in France after a successful battle with a submarine fleet. And a third speaks of the victorious advance of the troops of Democratic Russia, after the world had begun to believe that Russia had forgotten the War in her new freedom.

I read them over again, and I think that each one of these clippings, if true, writes "failure" once again upon the book of German diplomacy.

I remember a day not so very many months

The Complete Spy

ago, when a man with whom I had some business in—for me—less tranquil days, came to see me.

" B. E. is in town," he said quietly. " He says he must see you. Can you meet him at the —— Restaurant to-night? "

Boy-Ed! I was not surprised that he should be in America, for I knew the man's audacity. But what could he want of me? Well, it would do no harm to meet him, I thought, and anyway my curiosity was aroused.

I nodded.

"I'll be there," I said. " At what hour? "

" Six-thirty," my friend replied. " It's only for a minute. He is leaving to-night."

That evening for the first time in two years I saw the man who had done his best to compromise the United States. I did not ask him what his presence meant and, needless to say, he did not inform me.

Our business was of a different character. I had just arranged to write a series of newspaper articles exposing the operations of the Kaiser's secret service, and Boy-Ed tried to induce me to suppress them.

" I cannot do it," I told him.

But the captain showed a remarkable knowledge of my private affairs.

The Complete Spy

"Under your contract," he said, "the articles cannot be published until you have endorsed them. As you have not yet affixed your signature to them, you can suppress them by merely withholding your endorsement."

This I declined to do, and our conversation ended.

Shortly afterwards Boy-Ed returned to Germany on the U53. He did not attempt to see me again, but three times within the following weeks attempts were made on my life. Later, pressure was brought to bear from sources close to the German Embassy, but they failed to secure the suppression of the articles.

But my curiosity was aroused as to the meaning of Boy-Ed's presence, and I set to work to discover the purpose of it. This was not difficult, for although I have ceased to be a secret agent, I am still in touch with many who formerly gave me information, and I know ways of discovering many things I wish to learn.

Soon I had the full story of Boy-Ed's latest activities in the United States.

He had, I learned, gone first to Mexico in an attempt to pave the way for that last essay at a Mexican-Japanese alliance, which the discovery of the famous Zimmermann note later made

The Complete Spy

public. Whether he had succeeded or no I did not discover at the time. But, what was more important, I did learn that while he was in Mexico Boy-Ed had selected and established several submarine bases for Germany! His plans had also carried him to San Francisco, to which he had gone disguised only by a moustache. There he had identified several men who were needed by the counsel for the defence of the German Consul Bopp, who had been arrested on a charge of conspiring to foment sedition within the United States.

From the Pacific coast Boy-Ed had gone to Kansas City and had bought off a witness who had intended to testify for the United States in the trial of certain German agents. Thence, after a private errand of his own, he had made his way to New York, *en route* to Newport and Germany.

It may be well here to comment upon one feature of the Zimmermann note which has generally escaped attention. It was through no blunder of the German Government that that document came into the possession of the United States, as I happen to know. I must remind you that diplomatic negotiations are carried through in the following manner. The preliminary negotiations

The Complete Spy

are conducted by men of unofficial standing, and it is not until the attitude of the various Governments involved is thoroughly understood by each of them that final negotiations are drawn up. Now, although no negotiations had taken place between Germany, Japan and Mexico, the form of the Zimmermann note would seem to indicate that there was a thorough understanding between these countries. They were drawn up in this form with a purpose. Germany wished the United States to conclude that Mexico and Japan were hostile to her; Germany had hoped that America would be outwardly silent about the Zimmermann note, but would take some diplomatic action against Mexico and Japan which would inevitably draw these two countries into an anti-American alliance.

Did President Wilson perceive this thoroughly Teutonic plot? I cannot say; but, at any rate, upon February 28 he astounded America by revealing once again Germany's evil intentions towards the United States, and by so doing not only defeated the German Government's particular plan, but effectively cemented public opinion in the United States, bringing it to a unanimous support of the Government in the crisis which was slowly driving towards war.

The Complete Spy

That marked the last stand of German intrigue as it was conducted before the war. Now there is a new danger—a danger whose concrete illustration lies before me in the account of that first engagement between United States warships and German submarines.

The people of the United States, just entered into active participation in the War, are faced with a new peril—the betrayal of military and naval secrets to representatives of the German Government working in America. Not only was it known to Germany that American troops had been sent to France, but the very course that the transports were to take had been communicated to Berlin. It is probable that other news of equal value has been or is being sent to Germany at the present time; and the United States is confronted with the possibility of submarine attacks upon its troopships, as well as other dangers which, if not properly grappled with, may result in serious losses and greatly hamper it in its conduct of the War.

What exactly is this spy peril which the United States now faces and which constitutes a far greater, because less easily combated, danger than actual warfare?

How can it be got rid of?

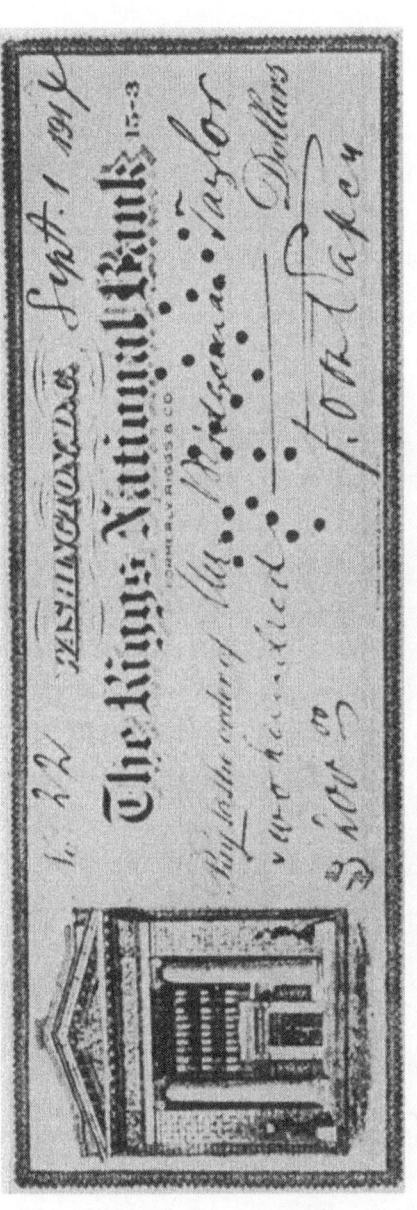

THE CHEQUE WHICH ALMOST COST CAPTAIN VON DER GOLTZ HIS LIFE (*See p. 193*)

The Complete Spy

These are the questions which the American people and the American Government are asking themselves and must ask themselves if they are to bear an effective share in the War in which they are engaged.

Because of my former connection with the German Government and my work as a secret agent both in Europe and America, in the former of which I was brought into intimate contact with the workings of the secret service in other countries, I am prepared to give an accurate account of the general structure and workings of the German spy system in the United States as it is to-day.

It is important to remember that the secret diplomatic service, as it was conducted in America before the War, and with which I was connected, is entirely different both in its personnel and methods from the spy system which is in operation to-day. I shall point out presently why this is so and why it must be so.

Before the entry of the United States into the War the principal activities of the German Government's agents were confined to the fomenting of strikes in munitions plants and other war activities, the organising of plots to blow up ships, canals, or bridges—anything which would hamper the transportation of supplies to

The Complete Spy

the Allies—and the inciting of sedition by stirring up trouble between German-Americans and Americans of other descent. All of these acts were committed in order to prevent the United States from aiding in any way the enemies of Germany; and also, by creating disorder in peace time, to furnish an object lesson of what could be done in time of war.

These things were planned, supervised and executed by Germans and by other enemies of the Allies, under the leadership of men like von Papen, who were accredited agents of the German Government and who were protected by diplomatic immunity.

Now that War has come an entirely new task is before the German Government and an entirely new set of people are needed to do it. War-time spying is absolutely different from the work which was done before the War, and the two have no connection with each other—except as the work done before the War has prepared the way for the work which is being done now.

And whereas the work done before the War was conducted by Germans, the present work, for very obvious reasons, cannot be done by anyone who is a German or who is likely to be suspected of German connections.

The Complete Spy

I venture to say that not 1 per cent. of the persons who are engaged in spying for the German Government at the present time is either of German birth or descent.

I say this, not because I know how the German secret service is being conducted in the United States, but because I know how it has been conducted in other countries.

Let me explain. It is obvious that such activities as the inciting to strikes and the conspiring which were done in the last three years could be safely conducted by Germans, because the two countries were at peace. The moment that War was declared every German became an object of suspicion, and his usefulness in spying—that is, the obtaining of military, naval, political and diplomatic secrets—was ended immediately. For that reason Germany and every other Government which has spies in the enemy country make a practice during War of employing virtually no known citizens of its own country.

At the present time more than 90 per cent. of the German spies in England are Englishmen. The rest are Russians, Dutchmen, Roumanians—what you will—anything but Germans.

One of the former heads of the French secret service in America was a man who called himself

The Complete Spy

Guillaume. His real name is Wilhelm and he was born in Berlin!

For that reason to arrest such men as Carl Heynen or Professor Hanneck is merely a precautionary measure. Whatever connection these men may have had with the German Government formerly, their work is now done, and their detention does not hinder the workings of the real spy system one iota.

HOW THE SPY SYSTEM WORKS

It is difficult to distinguish between the work done in neutral countries by the secret diplomatic agent—the man who is engaged in fomenting disorders, such as I have described—and the spy who is seeking military information which may be of future use. The two work together, in that the secret agent reports to Berlin the names of inhabitants of the country concerned who may be of use in securing information of military or naval value. It is well to remember, however, that the real spy always works alone. His connection with the Government is known only to a very few officials, and is rarely or never suspected by the people who assist him in securing information. Here permit me to make a distinction between two classes of spies: the agents or directors

The Complete Spy

of espionage, who know what they are doing; and the others, the small fry, who procure bits of information here and there and pass it on to their employers, the agents, often without realising the real purpose of their actions.

In the building of the spy system in America Germans and German-Americans have been used. Business houses—such as banks and insurance companies, which have unusual opportunities of obtaining information about their clients, most of whom, in the case of German institutions in America, are of German birth or descent—have been of service in bringing the directors of spy work into touch with people who will do the actual spying.

The German secret service makes a point of having in its possession lists of people who are in a position to find out facts of greater or less importance about Government officials. Housemaids, small tradesmen, and the like, can be of use in the compiling of data about men of importance, so that their personal habits, their financial status, their business and social relationships become a matter of record for future use. These facts are secured, usually by a little "jollying" rather than the payment of money, by the local agent—a person sometimes planted in

The Complete Spy

garrison towns, State capitals, etc.—who is paid a comparatively small monthly sum for such work. This information is passed to a director of spies, who thereby discovers men who are in a position to supply him with valuable data and who determine whether or not they can be reached.

Now, just how is this "reaching" done? Mainly, I think it safe to say, by blackmail and intimidation. If from this accumulated gossip about his intended victim—who may be an army or naval officer, a manufacturer of military supplies, or a Government clerk—the spy learns of some indiscretion committed by the man or his wife, he uses it as a lever in obtaining information that he desires. Or he may hear that a man is in financial straits. He will make a point of seeing that his victim is helped, and then will make use of the latter's friendship to worm facts out of him. In this way, sometimes without the suspicion of the victim being aroused, little bits of information are secured, which may be of no importance in themselves, but are of immense value when considered in conjunction with facts acquired elsewhere.

Ultimately the victim will jib or become suspicious. Then he is offered the alternative of

The Complete Spy

continuing to supply information or of being exposed for his previous activities. Generally he accepts the lesser evil.

In this manner the spy system is built up even in peace times. The tremendous sums of money that are spent in this manner amount to millions. The quantity of information secured is, on the other hand, inconceivably small for the most part. But in the mass of useless and superfluous facts that are supplied to the spies and through them to the Government, are to be found a few that are worth the cost of the system. By the time war breaks out, if it does, the German Government has in its possession innumerable facts about the equipment of the army and navy of its enemy—and, more important still, it has in its power men, sometimes high in the confidence of the enemy Government, who can be forced into giving additional information when needed.

Now, the moment that war breaks out, what happens? The German Government has, distributed throughout the country, thousands of men and women who have legitimate business there; it has its hands on men who are not spies, but who will betray secrets for a price either in money or security; it is acquainted with the strength and weakness of fortresses, various

The Complete Spy

units of the service, the exact armament of every ship in the Navy, the resources of munition factories—in a word, almost all of the essential details about that country's fighting and economic strength. It also knows what portion of the populace is inclined to be disaffected. And it is thoroughly familiar with the strategical points of that country, so that in case of invasion it may strike hard and effectively.

What it must learn now is:

First, what are the present military and naval activities of the enemy.

Second, what they are planning to do.

Finally, the German Government must learn the how, why, when and where of each of these things.

That, with the machinery at its command, is not so difficult as it would seem.

Here is where the value of the minor bits of information comes in. A trainman tells, for instance, that he has seen a trainload of soldiers that day, upon such and such a line. A similar report comes in from elsewhere. Meantime another agent has reported that a certain packing house has shipped to the Government so many tons of beef; while still another announces the delivery at a particular point of a totally different

The Complete Spy

kind of supplies. Do you not see how all these facts, taken together, and coupled with an accurate knowledge of transportation conditions and of the geographical structure of the country would constitute an important indication of an enemy's plans, even failing the possession of any absolute secrets? Do you not suppose that weeks before you were aware that any United States soldiers had sailed for France, the Germans might have known of all the preparations that were being made and could deduce accurately the number of troops that were sailing and many facts of importance about their equipment? There is no need for the betrayal of secrets for this kind of information to become known. It is a mere matter of detective work.

But mark one feature of it. These facts are communicated by different spies—not to a central clearing-house of information in the United States, as has been surmised, but to various points outside the country for transmission to the Great General Staff. They are duplicated endlessly by different agents. They are sent to many different people for transmission. *And even if half of the reports were lost, or half of the spies were discovered, there would still be a sufficient number left to carry on their work successfully.*

The Complete Spy

Germany does not depend upon one spy alone for even the smallest item. Always the work is duplicated. Always the same information is being secured by several men, not one of whom knows any of the others; and always that information is transmitted to Berlin through so many diverse channels that it is impossible for the most vigilant secret service in the world to prevent a goodly part of it from reaching its destination.

How that information is transmitted I shall tell in a moment. First I wish to explain how more important facts are secured—the secret plans of the Government, such, for instance, as the course which had been decided upon for the squadron which carried the first American troops to France.

It is obvious that such facts as these could not have been deduced from a mass of miscellaneous reports. That secret must have been learned in its entirety. Exactly how it was discovered I do not pretend to know, nor shall I offer any theories. But here, in a situation of this sort unquestionably, is where the real spy—the "master spy," if you wish to call him so—steps in.

Now, it is impossible, in spite of the utmost

The Complete Spy

vigilance, to keep an important document from the knowledge of all but one or two people. No matter how secret, it is almost certain to pass through the hands of a number of officials and possibly several clerks. And with every additional person who knows of it the risk of discovery or betrayal is correspondingly increased. If in code, it may be copied or memorised by a spy who is in a position to get hold of it, or by a person who is in the power of that spy! Once in Berlin, it can be deciphered. For the General Staff and the Admiralty have their experts in these matters who are very rarely defeated.

You may be sure that Germany has made her utmost efforts to put her spies into high places in America, just as she has tried to do elsewhere. You may be sure, also, that she has neglected no opportunity to gain control over any official or any naval or army officer—however important or unimportant—whom the agents could influence. That has always been her method; nor is it difficult to see why it frequently succeeds.

Imagine the situation of a man who in time of peace had supplied, either innocently or otherwise, a foreign agent with information which possessed a considerable value. It is probable

The Complete Spy

that he would revolt at a suggestion that he should do it in time of war—but with his neck once in the German noose, with the alternative of additional compliance or exposure facing him, it is not hard to see how some men would become conscious traitors and others would be driven to suicide.

By a system of blackmail and intimidation the Germans have attempted to force into their ranks many people from whom they extort information that would now be regarded as traitorous, although formerly it might have been given out in all innocence.

Undoubtedly it was for purposes of intimidation that von Papen carried with him to England papers incriminating Germans and German-Americans who had been associated with him in one way or another. And why did von Rintelen return to America and aid the Government in exposing the German connections of people who had no German blood in them? The obvious answer is that those people had refused to aid him in some scheme he had proposed. Therefore he made examples of them, with the double purpose of demonstrating to the United States the extent of German intrigue and of filling other implicated people with fear of the exposure that would come to them if they were not more compliant.

The Complete Spy

Once in possession of secret information, the spy is faced with the necessity of transmitting it to Berlin. Here again the spy who is a German would meet with considerable difficulty. He may mail letters if no mail censorship has been instituted; but these are liable to seizure and are not so useful in the transmission of war secrets as they were in informing his Government before the war of more or less standard facts about the strength of fortifications and the like. He may use private messengers—as do all spies—but the delay in this method is a severe handicap.

In sending news of the movements of troops speed is the prime essential. Consequently he must communicate either by wireless or by cable. How does he do it?

There are innumerable ways. There may be in the confidential employ of many business houses which do a large cable business with neutral countries men who are either agents or dupes of the German Government. These men may send cables which seem absolutely innocent business messages, but which if properly read impart facts of military value to the recipient in Holland, say, or in Spain, or South America. It is not a difficult matter to use business codes, giving to the terms an entirely different meaning from the one

The Complete Spy

assigned in the code-book. Personal messages are also used in this way, as is well known. As to the wireless, although all stations are under rigid supervision, what is to prevent the Germans from establishing a wireless station in the Kentucky mountains, for instance, and for a time operating it successfully?

But in spite of all cable censorship, the spy can smuggle information into Mexico, where it can be cabled or wirelessed on to Berlin, either directly or indirectly by way of one of the neutral countries. Even in spite of the most rigid censorship of mails and telegrams this sort of smuggling can be accomplished.

When I was in the Constitutional Army in Mexico I used to receive revolver ammunition from an old German who carried it over the border *in his wooden leg*. Could not this method be applied to dispatches?

There are numerous authenticated cases of spies who have sent messages concealed in sausages or other articles of food. Moreover, the current of the Rio Grande at certain places runs in such a manner that a log or a bucket dropped in on the American side will drift to the Mexican shore and arrive at a point which can be determined with almost mathematical precision.

The Complete Spy

I mention these instances merely to show how little of real value the censorship of cables and mails can accomplish. The question arises: What can be done? I shall try to indicate the answer.

HOW TO GET RID OF THE SPY SYSTEM

I say frankly that I think it absolutely impossible to eradicate spies from any country. Certainly it cannot be done in a week or a year, or even in many years. It is more than probable that the German spy systems in France and England are more complete to-day than they were at the beginning of the War. Three years ago the spies in these countries were made up of both experienced and inexperienced men. Now the bunglers have been weeded out, and only those who are expert in defying detection remain. But these are the only men who were ever of real use to Germany; and fortified as they are by three years of unsuspected work in these countries, they are enabled to secure information of infinitely more worth than they formerly were.

What is the situation in America?

I have shown you the structure of that system. Let me repeat again that Germany has installed in America thousands of men whose nationality

The Complete Spy

and habits are such as to protect them from suspicion, who work silently and alone, because they know that their very lives depend upon their silence, and who are in communication with no central spy organisation, for the very simple reason that no such organisation exists. There is no clearing-house for spy information in the United States. There are no "master spies."

Do you think that the German Government would risk the success of a work so important as this by organising a system which the arrest of any one man or group of men would betray? The idea of centralisation in this work is popular at present. In theory it is a good one. In practice it is impossible. By the very nature of the spy's trade he must run alone, and not only be unsuspected of any connection with Germany now, but be believed never to have had such a connection. If the secret service were a chain, the loss of one link would break it. With a system of independent units, endlessly overlapping, eternally duplicating each other's work, they continue their practices even though half of their number are caught.

Now with these men, protected as they are by the fact that not even their fellows know them, with their wits sharpened by three years of silent

The Complete Spy

warfare against the agents of other Governments and the American neutrality squad, the task of ferreting them out is an utterly impossible one. You cannot prevent spies from securing information.

You cannot prevent the transmission of that information to Berlin without instituting, not a censorship, but a complete suppression of all communications of any sort.

But you can do much to counteract their methods by doing two things:

I. Delaying all mails and cables, other than actual Government messages.

II. Instituting a system of counter-espionage, which shall have for its object the detection *but not the arrest* of enemy spies; and the dissemination of misleading information.

The war work of the spy depends for success upon the speed with which he can communicate new facts to Berlin. If all his messages are delayed his effectiveness is severely crippled.

If, in addition to that, all persons sending suspicious messages anywhere are carefully shadowed; if their associations are looked up, it may be possible to determine from whom they are getting information, and by seeing that incorrect reports

The Complete Spy

are given them, render them of negligible value to their employers.

Public arrests of suspected men are worthless. Such disclosures only serve to put the real spies on their guard. But if the spies are allowed to work in fancied security, it will be possible to find out just what they know, and the Government can change its plans at the last moment and so stultify their efforts.

Eternal vigilance, here as elsewhere, is the price of security. Germany has regarded the work of her spies as of almost as much importance as the force in the field. She has spent millions of dollars in building up a system in America whose ramifications extend to all points of its national life. And since upon this system rest all her hopes of rendering worthless American participation in the war, she will not lightly let it fail.

I toss aside my clippings and sit looking out into the New York street which shows such little sign of war as yet. Defeat! That is the end of this silent warfare, this secret underground attack that has in it nothing of humanity or honour. I think of Germany, a country of quiet, peaceful folk as I once knew it, bearing no malice, going cheerfully about their work, seeking their destiny with a will that has nothing in it of conquest. And I

The Complete Spy

think of Germany embattled, ruled by a group of iron men who seek only their own ambitions as a goal—who have brought upon the country and the world this three-years' tyranny of hate.

What will be the end? Will the war go on, eating up the lives and honour of men with its monstrous appetite? Or will there be peace—a peace that will bring nothing of revenge or oppression; that will carry with it only a desire for justice to all the peoples of the earth—that will kill for ever this desire for conquest which now and in the past has borne only sorrow and bloodshed as its fruit? Will the peace bring forgetfulness of the past, in so far as men *can* forget?

That would be worth fighting for.

PRINTED BY
CASSELL & COMPANY, LIMITED, LA BELLE SAUVAGE,
LONDON, E C 4
F. 30. 218

www.ingramcontent.com/pod-product-compliance
Lightning Source LLC
Chambersburg PA
CBHW032124160426
43197CB00008B/509